Ripples of Suicide

RIPPLES of SUICIDE

Reasons For Living

By Harold Elliott with Brad Bailey
FOREWORD BY ART LINKLETTER

WRS
PUBLISHING

A Division of WRS Group, Inc.
Waco, Texas

First published in the United States of America in 1993 by WRS Publishing, A Division of WRS Group, Inc., 701 N. New Road, Waco, Texas 76710
Book design by Kenneth Turbeville
Jacket design and photo manipulation by Joe James

10 9 8 7 6 5 4 3 2 1

Library of Congress Cataloging-in-Publication Data

Elliot, Harold, 1935-
    Ripples of suicide : reasons for living / by Harold Elliot with Brad Bailey ; foreword by Art Linkletter.
        p.   cm.
    Includes bibliographical references.
    ISBN 1-56796-012-X : $12.95
    1. Suicide victims—United States—Family relationships. 2. Suicide—Psychological aspects. 3. Bereavement—Psychological aspects.
4. Suicide—Religious aspects—Christianity. I. Bailey, Brad, 1953-   .
II. Title.
HV6546.E44 1993
362.2'8—dc20
    [B]
                                                            93-27775
                                                                CIP

I dedicate this book to my wife, Norma.

—*Harold Elliott*

Foreword

The word "suicide" is without doubt one of the most dreadful expressions in the English language.

People wince at the sound of it, and avoid using it to describe the tragic death it implies. Leprosy and Cancer are spoken of in the same hushed tones.

And yet it must be faced squarely and discussed openly because it has become one of the leading causes of death among both the young and the very old in this country.

No one can be sure of the exact figures because suicides are deliberately mis-reported and mis-diagnosed as an accident.

My own personal experience with it is still a nightmare. The death of my nineteen-year-old daughter, Diane, after experimenting with LSD, changed my life and the lives of everyone in my family. We still find it difficult to understand or discuss.

Since then I have counseled with many grieving parents who have sought me out because they know that only those who have experienced this loss can understand its depth and its consequences in a family.

We need to know more about the complexity of the decision to take one's own life, and Harold Elliott writes movingly and sympathetically and knowledgably about the "how's" and "why's."

During these turbulent times for the American family, when children are whip-sawed by life's frustrations and hopeless expectations, we desperately need this real-life knowledge of a growing tragedy.

Mr. Elliott has seen it all. He reports it with great understanding. He makes many positive and constructive comments about it. I congratulate him on this tremendous contribution to our society.

—Art Linkletter

Chapter 1

Along with a steady diet of murders and fatal accidents, as chaplain of the Arlington, Texas, Police Department, I had seen suicides galore.

I had been on the scenes of innumerable hangings, self-inflicted gunshot wounds, vehicular suicides, overdoses—the full gamut of Self's inhumanity to Self. I had wiped brains off my shoes, and had my clothes contaminated with the unerasable stench of extended decomposition.

But until April 1983, I guess I'd never really *seen* these suicides at all—had tried hard *not* to really see them, in fact.

That's the reason I sometimes come back out to a scene like this one, out by this little hill on the east side of town. I just sit here in the car, remembering, until my mind's eye begins to focus on that day, and I begin to actually feel the bumpiness as the squad cars lurch across the field; feel the apprehension even though we already knew what we'd find...

Except that I found something different that day.

People who don't know me well may be tempted to believe that my interest in suicide prevention is actually morbid and gruesome—an excuse to immerse myself in "gory details." And there are indeed some things in my desk down at the police station that can make strong stomachs turn and grown men pale. But in order to talk to people about suicide, I have to be able to remember details of particular suicides and the lessons contained therein. In my prior thirty years as a Baptist pastor, I had developed a pretty good memory for putting names with faces. But that hasn't helped me much here at the Arlington Police Department, because the problem with names and faces in my second career is this: A lot of times the people I work with don't have faces anymore. Many times they don't even have heads. And if they've been out in the elements—subjected to the heat and the insects—for any length of time, sometimes they don't have very much of anything at all.

So, lacking faces, I put the names with the crime-scene photographs. "Oh yeah," I'll say, "that was so-and-so. Used a thirty-ought-six. It was as messy as it looks," or, "That was such and such. He was gone for three weeks before they found him."

Even fellow professionals who see these grim last portraits of a life gone as wrong as it can possibly go sometimes have trouble facing the brutal slush of these photographs. They pick them up carefully, reluctantly, but their sense of "macho" forces them to look, whether they like it or not. They think, if this *preacher* can take it, so can I.

But they really don't want to look. I don't want to look either, really, except that it's part of my job. And that general unwillingness to look is a small reflection of a much larger truth: I have learned that society doesn't want to look, either.

It's ironic to me that, in an age when anything goes (or at least, *talk* about anything goes), there remains one subject we compulsively sweep under the rug: suicide. We hide it behind reconstructive mortuary techniques and obituary notices that neglect to mention causes of death. And we glorify the public's perception of it with pretty, ennobling, dangerous myths like that of Romeo and Juliet. We use platitudes like, "He's not suffering any more," or "He's out of it now." (Never mind the fact that he's plunged his family into a Hell on earth!)

For each individual suicide, this tendency to euphemize and eulogize is, of course, simple charitable mercy. I have preached more than my share of these memorial services. Out of deference to the living, *of course* I have nothing harsh to say of the dead or about the foolishness with which they acted in killing themselves. Sometimes I wonder, though, whether I'm helping the problem to persist by performing these platitudinous obsequies. Because as long as we, as a society, keep hiding the ugly, terrible truth, people will keep on killing themselves. It's happening now in greater numbers than ever, in ways that are horrific to behold, and for rationales that almost never stand up to the light of reason.

Part of the reason is simple ignorance of the subject. Most people don't know the signs of suicide, don't know what causes suicide, and don't see any real reason to learn. After all, it's a pretty unpleasant subject. Part of this unpleasantness is its finality, which leaves people feeling vaguely hopeless. The other problem is that there is no cure for it. You can prevent it. But you sure can't cure it.

Yet the biggest obstacle is simply the belief that it can't happen to *me*. It can't happen to *mine*. You have to be crazy to kill yourself. I am not crazy. Therefore, what's it to me?

For a long time, I felt the same way—what's it to me? It's sad, it's tough, but it doesn't have anything to do with me after I go home. So I didn't really see. I didn't want to.

Early on, at the scenes, I learned to defend myself against the dead, and to help defend my officers from the dead as well. In fact, if you do *not* defend yourself psychologically, odds are you'll go mad—or kill yourself. Suicide rates among policemen are higher than the norm. The extent to which he or she can isolate this grisly and hopelessly negative business from the rest of the mostly kinder, mostly gentler, and mostly still-hopeful world is the extent to which an officer can remain "normal" and capable of human feeling.

One *must* depersonalize, even dehumanize, the deserted husks remaining after life has either fled or, in suicide cases, sent itself packing. Neither police officers nor their chaplains can *afford* to personalize every ravaged corpse they see day in, day out, on early, swing, and graveyard shifts. They have to fight personalization. Because the sad human truth is that, no matter how hard they fight, they will probably still wind up caring more than is good for them over the course of a long, hard, and often thankless career. They must save their emotion for the living, for those shattered survivors in the next room who are crying and asking themselves, "What did I do wrong?" These survivors may, without proper care, ask themselves that miserable gut-wrenching question for the rest of their lives.

My first violent death scene was nearly twenty years ago, and, still fresh from the protected environment of the pastor's study, I was nervous. I didn't know if I would be cool, calm, and collected, or if I would take one look and throw up or run screaming from the room. The officers standing guard in front of the house had troubled themselves to warn me, "Chaplain, you need to know. This is a *bad* one."

And it was bad even for a *bad* one. The murdered woman's boyfriend had stabbed her thirty times as she struggled, turning the room into a nightmarish abattoir. Some "boyfriend."

There was some initial shock and disbelief that one person could do this to another, but almost immediately, I stumbled onto the trick: I had to think of the corpses as wax figures, mannequins in a wax museum designed only to shock the ticket holder. (In a sense, that's not far from the truth; they are just a shell. The life has gone, taking who they were with it.)

And my first *suicide* scene may have also been the worst one, in terms of grisly gore. The man had actually called the police and told them that he was going to kill himself. We arrived outside the house at the moment he pulled the trigger. He used a shotgun. He blew his brains not only *out*, but also all the way down the hall and into the living room.

Officers hit the dirt with the sound of the initial blast, and then *stayed* down as bits of speeding skull peppered the walls. The officers mistook the bap-bap-bap-bap for gunfire.

I learned at that scene and hundreds of others that

when you see a dead body like that, particularly ones in such spectacular disrepair, you should see it as a wax figure from Madame Tussaud's and refuse to be shocked or manipulated by it.

You shouldn't look too long at a time, either.

At such a time, I don't deliberately force myself to think of other things, but I don't let my eyes linger. I look at the face, if there is one, as quickly and as forthrightly as possible, so that I can tell the family whether they'll ever be able to view their loved one again. I get the clothing information and the who-what-where-when-how of what happened, but I do not linger, and I do not dwell. And then I go to the family.

That's the hardest part. The body you're seeing is just a shell—unless it's the body of a friend, or a loved one, or someone who reminds you of someone you love—just a shell.

That's what I usually saw. Until April 1984, my "professionalism" blinded me from seeing anything more.

Standing here now, where it happened, I can see the scene as clearly in my mind as if it were yesterday. Apartments and the usual growing suburban sprawl have now encroached on this undeveloped acreage, but the little hill in the field of scraggly Texas brush remains as it was back then.

A team of surveyors, planning the very apartments and streets that are here now, kept noticing the pickup truck throughout most of the morning. It was down by a big tree at the base of the little flat-topped hill. The area was all much more isolated than it is now, and the pickup was several hundred yards from where a pickup ought to be. At first, they assumed it had been stolen and abandoned. But the thought kept nagging them: Why would the driver of a stolen truck go to such pains to cross a treacherous and brushy field and perhaps attract police? Why not just quickly park it at the curb and jump out and run?

At mid-afternoon they decided to go take a look.

They were sorry they did, because that's when they found the two boys.

I can still see the two of them, as clear as day. They both had on T-shirts and jeans. They were both slumped forward in the cab of the truck. And both had been shot in the head. In this particular case, the gun didn't do as much damage as is usual. (Normally, a gunshot at such close range can literally destroy a head, or a massive portion of it. Remember the Kennedy assassination film?)

But in this case, although there was considerable trauma, it didn't blow their features away.

Families of suicides find this fact almost disproportionately comforting. In the midst of all their pain, learning that sons or daughters or wives or husbands or fathers or mothers are still "viewable" may be the only small island of comfort in an otherwise overwhelming sea of pain.

In this case, it may have been the relative intactness of their faces that overpowered my "professionalism." Or perhaps the fact that it was my first multiple suicide. I had by then seen numerous suicides, even teen suicides. I had worked juvenile suicides involving my own family's friends. In fact, the son of one couple I'd known for years was the first adolescent suicide I'd worked.

But prior to this, there'd only been one at a time.

Perhaps the location also had something to do with my coming change in awareness. Death in an isolated place like this is death in the raw. There is a world of difference between a sterile death at Arlington Memorial Hospital or an embalmed death at Arlington Funeral Home and the hard, red, raw, uncut and uncensored death at the bottom of that lonely, forlorn, isolated hill.

In places like this it's Death with a Capital D—darker and more elemental, as if leathery wings and black claws and sharp teeth had indeed come scraping and slashing across this lonesome landscape the midnight before.

Here, death smells different.

It's not decomposition, that smell, nor blood, nor any of the other fluids that are released. Most police officers swear to it: In places like this, death has an unmistakable and inimitable odor. Once you've smelled it, you never forget it. Though often faint, it's the strongest reminder of your own frail mortality that you're ever likely to receive.

The medical examiner figured the two boys had been there only since after midnight, just hours before we got there. Later, I would to my dismay learn that there was absolutely nothing remarkable about these two boys—other than the fact that they'd killed themselves. There was nothing to set them apart, and thus there was nothing to set them at a remove from myself and other "normal" people.

They were average, ordinary young men who were neither exceptionally good nor exceptionally bad. I couldn't say that those boys were any different than ninety-nine percent of the other kids in Arlington or, for that matter, any other city or suburb in the United States.

They were neither overly popular nor universally disliked; in fact, I think they were probably about like I was when I was their age. They just seemed to be ordinary kids with ordinary working parents who were trying hard to keep it all going. They went to the same high school and were about the same age as my daughter, Tina.

Like Tina, they had the problems that any child of the late twentieth century faces. They, like Tina, were fighting that seemingly impossible, hopeless battle with adolescent hormones. They, like Tina, were living in an unpredictable world with no certain future, and in a present where, if life was not instantly gratifying, it was seen as unbearable.

Part of my job, the worst part, is to notify families of endings like these.

How does this feel? It is absolutely *crushing* to have to tell someone something like that. You know when you pull up in front of the house that you've been forced into the position of having to finish the destruction that someone else has already set in motion.

I've said to my wife, Norma, many times: "I'm having to go to these people, and I don't even know who they are. They're sitting there in their homes or lying in their beds at peace with the world. And I'm going to have to go in there and crush the very life out of them, and they'll never be the same. Never."

And there I was again.

As most of us would under similar circumstances, I had always tried to be superhumanly sympathetic to the survivors of these suicides.

One boy's mother worked just up the way from that sad field, at a K mart on Abram Road. I went into the store and asked the manager to call her into his office. She came in no more perplexed than any other employee suddenly summoned to the office. She feared getting fired, but what she got was far, far worse.

I told her who I was, and then as gently and yet as straightforwardly as possible, what had happened. I'll never forget what she said, as she crumpled into the first of many hopeless sobs: "Oh, he'll be back. He's done this before. He's gone out and stayed gone all night before. He'll be back."

And I found myself having to drive it in even harder: "No ma'am. Not this time. This time he's dead."

All you can do at these times is be a shoulder to cry on, and attempt to help them marshal their own support system of friends and intimates to help them begin that long, hard process of grieving and letting go.

Then I went to the other boy's home. There it was harder. She said, "He didn't even kiss me goodbye..."

And yet, as sad as it all was, I still hadn't made the connection.

Later that day, as I thought about those two dashed hopes slumping there in that truck, it hit me, as hard as I've ever been hit by anything in my life: But for the grace of God, that could *be* Tina. And those parents could be me.

That thought would change my life.

Chapter 2

An act like this is prepared within the silence of the heart, as is a great work of art.—Albert Camus

To someone who has never contemplated suicide—or, much more likely, someone who has contemplated it and dismissed it—the central cipher to the puzzle of suicide is always the reason. The field known as "suicidology" has only been around about one hundred years, and during that time there have been numerous psychological, sociological and statistical assays of suicide, in hopes of determining what that reason is.

The only answer seems to be that there isn't any "only" answer.

Some would argue that you'd have to be crazy to kill yourself—that no sane person would be capable of it, and therefore that everyone who does is suffering from mental illness. And it is true that in cases of quantifiable, diagnosable mental illness—those cases, in other words, where it was at least felt that psychological problems were extreme enough to merit professional attention—suicide rates are indeed high.

Schizophrenics sometimes kill themselves, particularly when they are plagued by feelings of unavoidable upcoming disaster, and, less frequently, under the influence of voices ordering them to do so, or to escape imagined persecutions. People with personality disorders, particularly hysterics with an insatiable and unrealistic longing for love and attention from others, may exploit the dramatic appeal and emotional impact of the suicidal act to meet their need to make a sympathetic appeal to others.

Psychopaths, with their strong aggressive impulses and irresponsibility, may turn those urges against themselves. Sufferers from chronic depressive illness, or what Freud called melancholia, have the highest suicide risk. Because of the associated profound pessimism, feelings of futility, guilt, self-reproach and worthlessness, depressives almost invariably wish for death, and many, though far from all, commit suicide.

But the "crazy" approach raises questions: who's doing the diagnosing, how broad is his definition, and how strong is his interpretive bias?

The high incidence of suicide in prison could be used to point to proof that psychopaths—and there are many in prisons—are suicide-prone. On the other hand, the horrors and monotonous futility of prison could cause anyone to seriously consider killing himself even if he were sane.

The question of depression further muddies the water. There is the classic depression of the clinical kind, which comes from no clear external cause. There is also the situational kind, such as results from a traumatizing loss— death or divorce, hopeless unemployment, and so on. Unfortunately, the surest way to diagnose the difference between a normal reaction to bad circumstances and an excessive reaction is that the person commits suicide. There is also the excessive depressive reaction to traumatic loss—of which suicide is sometimes a symptom.

It takes years and years of training to clearly and reliably sort out the three. Where does that leave the layman? In all too many cases, saying, "I should have seen it coming."

Which brings us around to the original question: Is the unhappy but seemingly normal person who kills himself crazy?

It has been shown statistically that only about a third of the people who commit suicide were suffering from a readily apparent neurosis, psychosis, or severe personality disorder at the time of their death. Subsequent investigation in some cases may reveal that some of the remaining two-thirds were probably not well-balanced personalities who could have benefited from psychiatric attention.

The point is it's a gray, gray area. Nobody is perfectly well-balanced. How can we know how imperfectly balanced we must be before we kill ourselves? And what factors may augment that imbalance and encourage suicide, or offset that imbalance and discourage it?

So the same thing that puzzles many survivors also puzzles the experts: Frequently the reasons given by the victims are sufficient for unhappiness, but are hardly ever so serious that suicide is the only reasonable alternative— to a normal person. And since conscious motives as stated by the suicide seem prima facie insufficient (to researchers, if not to the victim), researchers and theorists have seized on various hypotheses as *the* answer—although more likely each contains only a smidgen of truth.

The first large contribution to the field of suicidology was that of Emile Durkheim, whose *Le Suicide* was first published in 1897 (and, perhaps confirming the fledgling nature of the field, remained untranslated into English until 1952). Durkheim's work on the subject was groundbreaking because it swept the subject back out from under the rug of Victorian moral indignation and because it attracted other scientists into a discussion of an issue which had previously been almost exclusively the province of theologians and moralists.

Durkheim could be said to be the father of suicidology— but like all fathers, he had some shortcomings. Given the fact that he was foremost a sociologist, Durkheim held that suicide could and should be explained in social (or external) terms and contexts, in spite of the fact that suicide seems to be a highly individual, personal action. He held that a certain number of suicides could be expected in any given culture, and that faults in the structure of the culture led to increases in the rates. And an individual's susceptibility to these faults depended on the strength and nature of his relationship to the society.

About as far as he would go in admitting suicide's highly personal, highly individual and psychological element was to divide people who killed themselves into three broad categories—egoistic, altruistic, anomic. But he still asserted that each was merely the statistically predictable product of social factors.

The egoistic suicide, he said, occurred where there was an excess of individualism resulting from improper integration into society. In the simplest example, the egoistic suicide was the result of individuating influences like the disintegration of family life, wars, the decline of religion, and other social dysfunction and malaise.

Altruistic suicide, he held, was a result of the opposite dynamic, wherein a person became so completely absorbed in the surrounding social group's goals and identities that he was willing to die for them. Religious and political martyrs, such as the Buddhist monks who burned themselves to death in 1970 to protest the Christian majority's treatment of their religion, are perhaps the perfect case in point.

The anomic suicide resulted when society sneaked up on you, according to Durkheim. It stemmed from a sudden and uncontrollable change in one's social status, which removed the person from all familiar hierarchies and understandings. Where in egoistic suicide there is too little structure, and in altruistic suicide, too much, in anomic suicide, there is no familiar structure at all. The rich man who loses everything in the stock market crash or the poor man who wins millions in the lottery could both face the kind of ruthlessness Durkheim believed was responsible for the third kind of suicide.

Durkheim's scholarship was sound and his methods were proper, but, since they were both of the late eighteen hundreds, they were very little influenced by psychology. As a result, many of those sociologists who have followed him into the field have been somewhat intimidated by him, and have to a large extent managed to deaden the field.

The kernel of truth here seems to be that the degree of the person's social integration—whether married or unmarried, working or unemployed, surrounded by friends and family or all alone—seems to have some statistical correlation to suicide rates—but sociological interpretations alone do not answer the cart-before-horse question.

Oversimplifying for the sake of brevity, the questions are: Does one kill oneself because of poor social integration—or is one both poorly integrated and suicidal because of some underlying psychological condition? Does one wind up all alone, broke, depressed, and friendless in a tenement because of societally remediable factors, like income, or the failure of the church and family? Or does one wind up there because one is depressed and therefore unfriendly, unsociable, and unemployable?

As Alvarez put it in his masterful *The Savage God*:

Despair... seeks its own environment as surely as water finds its own level. Thus the sociological theories woven around suicide are all to some extent true... but they are also partial and circular. They return constantly to an inner negation and hopelessness which social pressures may bring to the surface but which existed before those pressures and probably will continue after they are removed.

The first real debates concerning the underlying psychodynamics of suicide began in 1910 among Sigmund Freud and his circle of associates. Some in his circle held that the urge to inflict pain and sorrow on relatives was central to the issue, and that the strength of one's "aggressive drive" was important. Others among the group contributed global theories that may now be viewed more as only possible parts of the whole—germane in some cases, inapplicable in others.

Among the varying hypotheses are the following: Nobody kills himself unless he also wanted to kill another, or at least wished some other person to die; nobody kills himself unless his death is also wished by another person; and only he who has given up hope to be loved gives up his life (this last rings truest for many).

Freud himself attempted to explain it with the idea of a "death instinct." He pondered whether this urge somehow existed side by side with the urge to preserve one's self and one's species.

The argument against this is that, given the already

transitory nature of life itself, what purpose would such an instinct serve? There are many happy people in whom the "death instinct" is not at all evident and certainly not dominant, yet death is guaranteed. Death instinct or no, life still kills you. Even Freud himself, late in life and consumed by cancer, seemed to question the death instinct—along with much of the rest of his life's work.

Then there is the question of the "death trend," which is particularly disturbing for children of suicides. In examining fifty attempted suicides, two psychiatrists discovered that in ninety-five percent of them there had been the loss of a parent, sibling, mate or "significant other" under tragic circumstances, and that in seventy-five percent of these cases, the deaths occurred before the suicide-prone individuals had completed adolescence.

Many other studies have echoed those findings.

If, as some have suggested, suicidal fantasies represent a form of problem-solving behavior, this may offer clues as to why one person with these fantasies will act on them, while another will not. They may think, if it was good enough for Mom, it's good enough for me.

If there does exist a death trend or some instinct urging one toward death in spite of the urge toward life, many believe that the thing that allows Death to overcome the balance, the central enabling mechanism of suicide, is that the human mind has great difficulty conceiving of its own nonexistence. This seemingly rock-solid delusion of immortality may allow the sufferer to conceive of suicide as a means of shedding the destructive elements, the demons inside him, and thus be transported into a better "life." In this case, the taking of one's own life is seen as self-empowerment rather than the ultimate end of self and thus the end of power; as an assumption of control rather than the complete and final abdication of it. Then and only then can suicide be seen as an alternative, rather than truly as the end of alternatives.

It can be shown and argued that some sociological and psychological factors do have a bearing on suicide. More suicides come from broken homes, so it could be argued that a broken home creates the kind of emotional and social instability that can predispose a person to the kind of problems which can end in suicidal crises.

But how imperfect must the personality's balance be before suicide is an option? How dysfunctional the relationship? How dominant and abusive the superego? How egoistic, altruistic or anomic the situation? How broken the home? It all depends on what you believe about death.

In the vast majority of cases, your belief about death and what happens after it is what makes the ultimate difference between pulling the trigger and living to find other cures for one's personal "demons."

Consider the maidens of Miletos. According to Plutarch, the girls were experiencing one of those strange epidemic outbreaks of suicide. They were rushing in disquieting numbers to hang themselves—until one of the locals suggested "shaming" their bodies by carrying them through the marketplace, which the surviving damsels decided "just would not do." The suicide epidemic stopped.

The only difference here, since nothing else had happened in their lives, was that someone changed their perception of death and what would happen to them afterwards.

Suicide is a volitional act. Volitional acts aim not merely at creating an effect, or even a specific effect, but also an observable effect. The unfortunate delusion in suicide, though, is that the suicidal person expects to observe the effect of his final act.

That is why suicide notes are far and away the most interesting documents you'll ever read, not so much because of what they contain, but because of what they are: The last recorded thoughts and musings of an individual creation of God about to render itself forever extinct by choice. Someone who obviously has something he needs to say only moments before entering eternity.

When you ponder the power of the survival instinct instilled in us, the fact that these remarkable notes exist make them as amazing as unicorns—and they exist in incredible numbers.

I have to admit that, after nearly twenty years of looking at them, these notes still unsettle me. The body at a suicide scene is after all, just that—a body, a shell. Whatever motivated it can be presumed to no longer exist, leaving it empty of thought and feeling. But the scribbles and screeds on ragged paper, the last record of that individual's distinct, unique and irreplaceable personality, these recorded thoughts hook us and reel us in like willing fish toward a larger mystery—what was that person thinking at the very last moment? At the instant the trigger was pulled?

There is in the generally available literature quite a bit about the "state of mind" of persons who have attempted suicide, but nothing specific about very last thoughts—and I suspect that I personally don't want to find it. On this one matter it may be more enlightening to speculate, because hard information would distract from the central question. The question is really not, what was that person thinking? The question is, What would *I* be thinking? How would the chain of my consciousness play itself out, pistol to my head, finger tightening on the trigger, and on what note would it end?

In print, I imagine it would read like a terribly incomplete sentence loaded with parenthetical expressions, reflecting a struggle for control between two sides of an ambiguous mind. This is, after all, the last battleground in a struggle between Life and Death. Death would by now have the upper hand, but Life, though weakened, would still be fighting to the very last, like a voice screaming from deep down inside a well: I (me???) am going to (this is crazy) do it this time (how *could* I) because I've had all (no, lost all) that I can take (maybe not) and I've just got to (don't got to do anything) do it *now* (No!)...

After that, only echoes rippling out into a world I can no longer hear, because the echoes move only among the living.

But the other thing about the notes giving me goose bumps on some occasions is not so much what they say, but just how little some say, under the awesome circumstances in which they were produced. Poised on the brink of the unknown and hard up against the wall of unarguable finality, one of our suicides wrote: "Changed the oil in the car. Put on new spark plug wires. The tank is full." This guy is dead all the way into the unforeseeable forever, and yet his last thoughts are of vehicle maintenance?

Most are not quite as terse, but many reveal a certain glib casualness that I find disconcerting; a sort of "oh, by the way, I'm about to kill myself" tone that always leaves me wondering whether the person felt that he was valued by no one, or merely failed to value himself. Most of all, they leave me wondering whether he understood the magnitude of the undertaking.

"Make sure everybody gets the presents that are in my closet," says this one in closing. Presents? This young man has just hit his family the hardest blow they'll ever receive, one they will never overcome—and he's playing Santa Claus?

There is no great evidence that suicide notes are more honest than other communications made under serious stress. Only about fifty percent may make reference to the actual motives for the suicide. And most seem to concentrate on events occurring—or emotions engendered—after the death.

Suicide experts generally divide the content of suicide notes into four broad categories.

1. Contrition. In this kind of note, the writer begs forgiveness, pleads that the problem was not of his own creation, and hopes that the reader will understand.

Here's one from a man who hanged himself; it reflects many of these themes.

I'm writing this today because if I wait until tomorrow I don't know if I'll be able to. I love you very much. I can't go on the way I have, I can't give you anything, in fact, I never have. I hope you go back to the family, I am sorry I ever took you away. If possible, I would like to be cremated and sprinkled in the mountains. I loved it up there, and wish I had never taken us away.

2. Illness. This is usually fairly straightforward. However, in this category here's a cautionary one:

I'm doing this by my own hand because death looks so good to me compared to the pain. Please do an autopsy to find the reason for the pain. I love you all.

The autopsy was done. There was nothing physically wrong with the man. There was no medical reason for physical pain—and if there were any discomfort, it had been produced by his emotions. Did this poor soul erroneously end himself because he believed he was dying—killed, in effect, by lack of a second opinion? In the strictest possible sense, a doctor could have saved his life.

The scary thing is that these self-diagnoses are not at all uncommon.

3. Spite. These are frequently bitter and punitive, designed to create guilt in survivors:

I got a new toy today, and I think this will finally make everybody happy. I wish you knew what it is like not to be loved. It is not good. I really don't have much to say that I haven't said already, except I love you more than you will ever know. PS, all the games are over.

The next one is little more than a quote from a record album, but like many, aims at showing that his death by his own hand was not his fault, but rather that of the world at large and its treatment of him:

Nobody can say it better than Pink Floyd:

Goodbye, cruel world, I'm leaving you today. Goodbye, goodbye, goodbye. Goodbye, cruel world, There's nothing you can say to make me change my mind... goodbye.

4. Last will and testament. These are generally very dry and straightforward, and include funeral and burial wishes. They communicate, if anything, the suicidal person's tendency toward bossiness, and perhaps intimate that the soon-to-be-deceased has feelings of omnipotence and plans to be there when the instructions are carried out.

Some researchers suspect that suicide notes may reflect

the mental and emotional efforts necessary for the suicide to overcome the societal taboo against suicide. To break these societal constraints, the potential suicide who is facing deeply distressing problems must also: see the situation as one in a long chain of similar crises; and think that death is the only way out; be unable to share his distress with others because of social isolation; suppress his belief that suicide is immoral or irrational, and succeeds in this because social isolation makes him feel less bound by societal strictures; rationalize so that he sees the problem as not of his own making and open to no other solution; and make some mental provision that the problem will not continue after his demise.

To me, perhaps the most infuriating aspect of suicide notes—the last communication to loved ones—is all the variations on the theme of "I'm sorry, forgive me, I love you, it's better this way." Infuriating, particularly to the survivor. If you are going to walk up to me and, for no apparent reason, double up your fist and hit me between the eyes with all your force, please do me the favor of not telling me you're sorry in advance. Don't ask me to forgive you for something you've planned to do. Don't tell me you love me and then hit me as hard as I can be hit.

And yet even these notes are touching. Not only can you feel some of the victim's pain shimmering up through that inanimate ink, but you can also feel that strange misplaced and unjustified optimism, the belief that the victim is going to feel lots better in just a minute, as soon as he pulls that trigger. He expects to continue to be concerned, post-existence, with how others will feel about what he has done. He seeks to direct the upcoming emotional response to what he has done, on the apparent assumption that he will be there—or five hundred feet up in the air—to relish it.

Equally as frightening is the fact that the notes frequently reveal vast illogic. Some people kill themselves out of what may simply boil down to faulty thinking— distorted thought processes of one kind or another. First and perhaps most dangerous is the type of thinking by

which judgments are made in terms of either/or, always/
never, good/bad, black/white, and life/death, with no
gradations or shades of gray.

These "allness terms," particularly the all/never
combination, frequently show up in the notes. Tests have
shown that suicidal people—those who have expressed a
strong desire to kill themselves, or those who have actually
attempted it—tend to think more in these terms than do
normal people or even those who are emotionally
disturbed but not suicidal.

Perhaps as important as this thinking, and closely
related to it, is a rigidity of thought. Rigid thinkers are
those who are incapable of changing their preconceived
ideas in spite of new facts and new information. Tests
have shown the suicide-prone to be rigidity-prone as well,
for perhaps obvious reasons. For instance, a rigid thinker
would be likely to form a permanent conclusion based
on only a few repetitions of unpleasantness. Then, in
spite of the fact that the unpleasantness was never again
repeated, this person would continue to believe that the
unpleasantness was always going to occur. It becomes
"the way things are," even if that's no longer really how
they are at all.

Another error researchers believe is present in some
suicidal thinking is the mistakenly ambiguous use of
certain terms, particularly in regard to the concept of
"self." The groundwork leading to suicide may be at least
partially laid by the person's confusing the "self" as he
personally experiences it with the "self" as experienced
externally, by other people and society at large. He may
think, "When someone kills himself, he gets attention.
Therefore, I will kill myself. And then I will finally get
some attention."

Researchers E. S. Schneidman and N. L. Farberow
explored this kind of thinking in their 1957 "Clues to
Suicide," writing, "...we believe that this kind of confusion
or ambiguity might indeed occur whenever an individual
thinks about his death, whether by suicide or otherwise.
It may arise because an individual cannot imagine his

own death, his own cessation of experience, a state where there is no more self as experienced by the self after death."

I see evidence of it all the time. It's crazy. And it's contagious.

Like so many other scenes of violence and self-destruction, I pass by it in traffic all the time. All these sites jog memories, but this one more than most. It's a concrete pylon supporting an overpass on a state highway. What makes it stand out—and jog my memory even more—is that big reddish-brown stain on the concrete, still visible after almost seven years.

A high-school student had been writing suicide notes, we later learned. (The notes had always said "we," so we wondered if the plan had been that he was going to take someone with him.) And he had told two of his friends of his plans before swearing them to secrecy. And, perhaps failing to take him completely seriously, they had honored that crazy, sad oath.

One morning before class he got into his pickup truck. It was really souped up—an old clunker he'd rebuilt from the ground up. And he said to some kids, "Think I'll see if I've got the nerve to do it." And he took off. Some of the other kids jumped in a car and followed him. Whether it is blood or just radiator rust that accounts for that stain on the pylon, I do not know, but the sixteen-year-old student was going one hundred mph when he hit it, and he hit it on purpose. Both he and the truck exploded.

This was in 1986. In Arlington, we'd already had our share of suicide crises—enough of them that we were ready with our response. When I addressed the student's fifth-period band class the next day, most of the kids already knew about his suicide. So I cut to the chase. I remember telling them, "I'm just as sorry as you are, but there's some things we need to talk about. You will go on to graduate, have husbands and wives, and he never will. If someone tells you they are going to take their life, for heaven's sake, don't keep it a secret."

A city council member was one of the first to reach the scene: he told students he'd pulled over and found the two distraught girls who'd chased him in the car.

"They were tore up, as all of you can imagine, and they handed me one of the suicide notes the boy had written," he said. "I've never felt so helpless in my life. There was absolutely nothing I could do."

Students clung to one another, sobbing. Throughout the day, they sought help in counselors' offices at the school, and support from the CARE group. We set up some time to let them ventilate their feelings, and there's a period of time where that's real; for the first hour, ninety-eight percent of it is real. The kids who were close to the victim come in and talk to us—they *need* to talk to someone; they don't understand their own emotions.

But after that, you begin to get... well, kids being kids. Some of the guys begin to see that it's a wonderful opportunity to hug all the girls who are crying. And some of the girls seem to be crying because they get hugged by all the boys. And you begin to wonder if some of these grieving kids haven't also found it to be a convenient way to get out of class. The grieving becomes a method of getting attention, and suddenly, everyone is the best friend of the deceased, even if they never said more than "Hello."

The problem here is, in that atmosphere, there's no way to tell who's faking and who really needs help. So when it begins to take on that carnival kind of atmosphere, the only thing you can do is shut it down. And wonder who you've missed.

Sometimes you get lucky and find them.

As I was leaving the school, I stopped off at a restroom. Standing there at the sink was a young man. He wasn't doing anything at all, just standing there. I looked a little closer. He was in a daze.

I asked him, "Are you all right?"

"Yes, I guess so..."

"Was he a friend of yours?... Let's go talk."

We sat down on a bench outside and talked for thirty minutes. Just talked. It was real. He just couldn't understand why it had happened: "How could he do something like this and not have *told* me anything?"

He felt betrayed by someone who had purported to be close, and then had done something like this. He started crying, and then he apologized for crying.

"It's all right," I assured him. "If Jesus could cry for Lazarus, you should certainly cry for your friend."

And a few days later, there was another chance.

There'd been some talk around the school that a girl had been acting strangely—remote, distracted. I like to credit the existence of CARE and the other programs for the kind of heightened awareness of potential "cluster" problems that caused them to watch her more closely, and may have saved her life.

Student concerns were confirmed and changed into full-fledged intervention when some of her classmates found her crying on a couple of occasions near the death scene. The second time they found her there, she told them she didn't want to live. She had been his girlfriend; I never could ascertain whether she was the other half of the "we" he had mentioned in his notes, but she was not in good shape. She told me also that she didn't want to live, that she was going to die, and that she wanted to be with him.

And I said, "Hold on—be with him *where*?"

"I don't know."

"Well," I asked, "Just where *is* he?"

"I don't know."

"Well, how do you know you want to be there? Listen. Let's say for purposes of illustration that you and I decide we don't want to be here. And we talk to your family, and we all decide we're just going to pack up and move five thousand miles west of here. Five thousand miles due west. What do you think we'll find there?"

"Why... I don't know."

"Well, I don't know either. It could be the middle of the ocean or a snake-infested environment, or nowhere at all, for all we know."

Every time there's a suicide in our school system—and there are fewer of them in Arlington these days—we make an immediate intervention. And the most difficult obstacle we encounter, time after time, is that people no longer seem to know about death what people my age knew when we were growing up. We were exposed to it, all the time. It would happen to a neighbor one week, and a relative the next. And we would see them, and know that dead means *dead*.

It is not some cop show lasting sixty minutes minus commercials where everybody dies dramatically and the same characters, more or less, return the following week, and all the actors show up in another series.

Dead means *dead*.

If this were just some isolated case of a poor immature little girl failing to think things through, it would still be cause for concern. She had shown that she was capable of considering permanent action on the basis of next to no information at all. And if we were to learn that there was some individual out there *encouraging* her to think that way, that would be cause for still more concern. That person would at least need to be clearly marked as a fount of misinformation and a major contributor to illogic before we allowed him to go traipsing around the school grounds.

Chapter 3

A patrolman and I were chatting in my office the other day, recalling what we both had to admit was a fairly typical youthful suicide of a few years earlier.

"Yeah," the officer said. "That was the one where the kid killed himself because his parents wouldn't let him go to the school dance. That's just plain dumb. I'm sorry, but I don't have any sympathy for someone like that."

Yes—dumb. And hard to understand—particularly for adults.

I am not here to convince anyone that I have the cure for suicide. On the contrary, I am here to state that it can happen to anyone, in any walk of life or socioeconomic circumstance. It can happen anytime, anywhere—and does. And before we can ever even begin to do anything about it, that fact *must* be acknowledged.

Even preachers are not immune to suicidal feelings.

Only people who have lived through that crazed phase of uncontrolled growth called "adolescence" (and, thankfully, that includes most of us) can look back upon the maddening maelstrom of conflicting feelings during these years and understand that it was only a tempest in a teapot. And a temporary, hormone-induced tempest at that.

But for most of us, there is no one to prepare us for that perilous crossing. Having long forgotten that precarious stage where the sting of every slight and the keenness of every longing is magnified and multiplied a hundredfold, tired parents disconnect by telling their kids that these are the best years of their lives. They thus leave them to find their own way through the minefield of mis-emotion, misunderstandings and misplaced ardor.

Being safely through it, parents may underestimate the potential for danger it holds for their offspring. They may lose sight of the wild impulsiveness and uncontrollability that holds sway during these years, along with a strong conviction that any action at all beats doing nothing. To a teen, everything needs doing right away.

I have worked suicides where young people have killed themselves for no greater *apparent* reason than that their parents wouldn't let them have the car for an evening. People shake their heads in disbelief and say, "I can't believe he'd kill himself over that," thus reaffirming their subconscious conviction that the suicide victim is simply crazy, different from Them and Theirs—and thus "proving" to themselves in the back of their minds that they're at less risk of ever doing it themselves.

But in this phase of life, the "reason" isn't really the reason at all.

In fact, as a teenager, I considered killing myself for perhaps not much more.

It was during that fragile time when I was trying to learn who Harold Elliott is—those early teenage years when new glands have gone haywire and it seems like the entire world thwarts you at every turn.

You are first enslaved by the paradox of the passions. Persons of the opposite sex are both compellingly attractive and yet complete conundrums, and you can't do anything about them—or about much of anything else, for that matter—because you are the Wrong Age, the Wrong Age Entirely. You're Entirely Too Old for this, and Just Too Young for the other. You know you're too old just to sit around at home with your parents, but you're not old enough to take the family car and go where you want to go, which is to wherever you can get into the most trouble. And even if you had one of your own, your daddy still tells you how, when, and where you can use it.

My "problems" were considerably complicated by the fact that, at the tender and amazingly ignorant age of fourteen, I had "received the call" to be a preacher—and had in fact already begun preaching.

Our little family in Clarendon, way out in West Texas, was not particularly religious—until a revival in 1949. That revival helped pave the way for my entering the ministry the following year.

The years have somewhat dimmed the memory. I can't recall exactly what it was the preacher was saying, only that it had a tremendous impact on me. It was as if God were talking directly to me, not in words, but to my heart. There was something He seemed to want me to do. And when the invitational came at the end of the service, my feet picked me up and moved me down the aisle.

Every head in the church turned in my direction. At first I was pleased by the attention. Then I got to wondering, what's the big deal? I'm just a kid. Then I realized they were staring not at me, but at a much more remarkable apparition in line just behind me—my father. It really must have been a *powerful* sermon.

Unbeknownst to me at the time, our family had something of a history of struggles with religion. My grandfather had felt very strongly that God had called him to the pulpit also. But he'd told God, "I can't. I have a wife and children I have to support, and so I just can't do it." And he truly believed he'd heard God then reply: "If that's your problem, I'll relieve you of that." Within something like a year, my grandmother and one of their children had died.

Did God do that? I personally doubt it. But Grandpa believed He did. And, perhaps predictably, instead of softening him, it hardened him for a period of years.

He was by all accounts pretty ornery, and had a terrible temper. But he finally gave in and went back to the fold.

And it was very ironic to me that on that May 14 he'd come all the way from Anderson County in deep East Texas to our far West Texas farm to spend the night.

We idolized that man. As far as we were concerned, his opinions contained both the wisdom of Solomon and the force of law. So as soon as I could get some time with him, I told him I felt very strongly that God was speaking to me, that he wanted me to preach. And I asked him:

"How do you surrender to preach?"

He said, "When the preacher gives the invitation, you go down the aisle and you tell the preacher that you feel like you've been called, and that you are surrendering your life to Christ."

And I replied: "When I get old enough, I'm going to do just that."

He said, "Well, how old *are* you?"

"Fourteen."

"If God calls you at fourteen, you're old enough."

And the next morning, a Sunday, I stood up in church and surrendered.

Looking back now, I suppose I'd do it all over again the same way. Believing, as we Baptists do, that God does indeed issue clear-cut calls, I'm not sure I even had the power to do otherwise. But I had sure put myself in a tight spot, and loaded myself with pressures few fourteen-year-olds have to face.

At any age, taking the step of entering the ministry sets you apart; at fourteen, all the more so.

There's a double standard people apply to preachers. People expect them to be pious, not particularly fun-loving, and completely immune to the pressures of the flesh. On anyone, that's a heavy weight. But on a fourteen-year-old, it's a terrible burden. It's not something you'd seek out.

I remember, for instance, one kid saying, "Well, you might as well be a preacher, 'cause you ain't fit for nothing else."

Already insecure, I was cut deeply by comments like that.

Then there was the simple fact that I didn't know *anything* about being a preacher, I had never even read the scriptures—and the week after I had surrendered, the pastor, who was not at all helpful, turned up the heat. He told me, "I think a preacher ought to preach, so I want you to preach next Sunday." I didn't know the first thing about it. I didn't have any books on the subject, and even if I'd had them, I wouldn't have known how to use them. So I went to him and said, "I need some help. How do you prepare a sermon?"

He just reached over, picked up a pile of old sermon outlines lying on his table and tossed them over and said, "Like that. And pray a lot."

That was my help. It was, in fact, for many years all the help I got. Only by the grace of God did I have a sermon—and it wasn't a particularly good one.

I can still, after all these years, feel what it was like— the apartness, the loneliness I faced. At other times I'd be filled with an overwhelming feeling of embarrassment over the presumptuousness of believing that the Lord had singled out a fourteen-year-old Clarendon farm boy to lead one of His flocks some day.

Saturday was the day the family usually drove into town; more and more of those Saturdays found me refusing to go. I didn't want to feel those eyes on the back of my neck and the possible whispers of, "So now the Elliott boy thinks he's a preacher, does he?"

I would rather have just stayed home by myself. I didn't want to see classmates who were no longer peers. Like most country kids, I'd been raised with a gun in my hand. And I'd take that old twenty-two rifle and go out and shoot at things. And there were times, many times, when I'd just sit down by the barn and think about my life and the strange and choking turns it had taken after my Call. And on one occasion, I leaned against the barn and said: "I can stop this. I could stop the hurting. I could stop the frustration."

Given my experiences in later years, I can pretty well envision what would have happened if I'd done it. First of all, everybody in Clarendon would have written me off as crazy. My mother would have been almost fatally saddened, I imagine, and my father would have been terminally humiliated.

But those aren't the things that stopped me.

The thing that kept me from it was almost as inane as my reasons for contemplating it in the first place: It was the thought of being in the ministry. "Preacher ought not do something like that," I thought, and so I didn't.

True, a preacher shouldn't (though they sometimes do), but there is something so flimsy and frail in those lines of logic—both reasons why and reasons why not— that scare me to this day. I'm not scared for myself; I got through this crazy, unpredictable, wrongheaded, and wildly impulsive phase. And having gone through it, now, as a suicide counselor, it helps me to remember something about young people. Whenever I want to think "That's dumb," I make myself go back to that time, there by the barn, and realize, *of course* it was dumb. What do we expect of people so young they have not yet learned how to live?

There are a lot of people out there who are still going through those years. Some of them might be yours. And more and more of our kids are killing themselves. Those two boys who shot themselves in the car in that lonely, isolated field were, sad to say, not isolated cases. Both the nation and our little part of it, the Dallas–Fort Worth area, were witnessing a dramatic increase in the numbers of youthful suicides in the early 1980s. National figures for suicides under age twenty-five had doubled since 1970, reaching six thousand a year by 1983.

In 1983 in the Dallas–Fort Worth area, eighty-one people under the age of twenty-five committed suicide. In 1970, only thirty-eight had made that fatal mistake.

There was—and is—a national preoccupation with suicide. This is alarming, but even more alarming is the tendency to "cluster" suicides—similar suicides occurring in one geographical area, and among members of a particular demographic, such as those in nearby Plano, where seven youthful suicides occurred in 1983. And even in small communities, like Sheridan, Arkansas, with a population of three thousand, where three young people had killed themselves. But Arlington, Texas, had perhaps the biggest problem of all: In that year, nine young people killed themselves.

Sad to say, part of the cause could be laid at the doorstep of Arlington's "success," if success is measured as growth.

The deaths occurred at the height of Sun Belt prosperity

and Rust Belt decline, when newcomers from all classes were crowding in for their slice of the city's prosperity pie. Where once we had been considered the conservative and comfortable bedroom-community buffer zone between Dallas and Fort Worth, we were now growing like mad. The population had exploded from one hundred thousand in 1970 to a quarter of a million in 1985. And where once we'd been considered steadfastly middle-class, we were now seeing an increased concentration of low-income families, with greater need for public health-care and social services. But the city was developing so quickly that civic officials were fighting just to maintain the basic services, like streets and sanitation, while fighting traffic congestion and—reactively more than proactively—waging war on crime.

There was no infrastructure in place to address the community's too-suddenly heightened awareness of youth suicide. As is frequently true, the results of the shortcomings and lack of vision of the adults were being visited upon children, whose problems were mounting almost geometrically.

By 1983, as many as two hundred young persons in the Dallas–Fort Worth area were being reported to police as "missing" each month. Most of these, of course, came home. But for others, horrible fates awaited. In the Dallas metro area, just as in any other major city, the kids would run away only to find someone who would exploit them. Horrible things like child porn and prostitution do happen. A lot of topless dancers are runaways under seventeen. So are many of the prostitutes.

To say that suicide is a symptom of other problems unnecessarily diminishes it. It's like saying that nuclear war is a symptom of poor diplomacy. As symptoms go, though, suicide's one of the more serious ones.

But in those days, we did have to acknowledge that suicide was a manifestation of the frustration that some of our young people were experiencing because of other problems. We knew that by remaining inactive we stood to lose part of a generation—but we didn't really quite know what to do about it. As is usual in communities stricken for the first time with so shocking a problem, we had nothing in place and no way to fight back. We floundered helplessly for a while, seeing the problem as immense and unsolvable. But then, as individuals, we began to find our way.

Each of us was on our own, each following our own insights into how to fight this war.

This approach—or lack of one—may have had some advantages, however, at least initially. Nobody felt hamstrung by the timidity of committees, because there weren't any, and nobody decided to "let George do it," because there *wasn't* a George. Operating independently and unaware of one another, we each took full responsibility for the breadth of the problem and addressed ourselves to curing it. (It was about then that I first began to toy with the idea of producing some kind of a video on the subject.)

But before the community could take any important action, it had to organize and define the problem, and its sources. I think the results of this process in Arlington could serve as a model for any city in the country. What Arlington has done on the subject of suicide is almost a contradiction in terms: We have created a level of bureaucracy that actually *works*.

And I would hasten to urge any community that does *not* have a system to help deal with this problem to develop one immediately, *before* they need it, because it's always already too late for someone.

After all, the two boys in that pickup were certainly not the first young suicides in Tarrant County. I know that perhaps better than anyone, and rather than point fingers of blame at the media, which many said were sensationalizing the situation, I can only extend my thanks and stand in shame for my earlier inactivity. The media made us look at the problems that were already there, made them high-profile enough to finally get onto our mental maps.

There had been some tentative stirrings in that direction

in the early 1980s. In an effort to identify problems stemming from the city's sudden growth, several Arlington citizens' groups did an in-depth "needs" study. The resulting publication, *Who's Minding the Children?* pointed out definite deficiencies in the child and family areas. To try to do something about these problems, concerned citizens organized the Arlington Human Services Project to serve as a continuing planning group and as an umbrella organization for specific social programs. AHSP's first major project was to establish an out-patient pediatric clinic in Arlington for low-income families, who are charged on a sliding scale according to their ability to pay.

After helping establish the pediatric clinic, volunteers initiated talks with officials of the Arlington school system about the need for after-school care for children. In the process, AHSP began to make important inroads and connections with the Arlington Independent School District that would be useful later on.

AHSP was enjoying growing clout and credence in the community when its path crossed that of suicide—thanks to Arthur Digby, senior minister at the First Christian Church in Arlington. Digby felt that, as individuals, people were greatly concerned by the growing suicide rate, but that they needed to organize and, to borrow a computer term, "defragment" that concern, to focus it and bring about some efficiency.

So Digby invited educators, counselors, parents, and civic leaders to discuss the increasing teenage suicide rate in the city. AHSP, Digby's group, and the school district all came together in a project called Youth Esteem Services, or YES.

These concerned citizens had the sensitivity to realize that adults could do far less about youth suicide than could the youths themselves, if properly organized and directed. This was because troubled young people are more willing to talk to other young people than to teachers, policemen, counselors, or, sad to say, their own parents.

Under YES, an administrator or teacher is chosen to develop what is called a "CARE Team" from the student body at each of Arlington's high schools and junior highs. "Egalitarian" is the watchword for this selection process. The teacher puts the emphasis not on who's popular or who's a good student, but on which kids the other kids seem to talk to. Care is further taken to ensure that there is at least one representative of each of the sub-demographics that students tend to divide themselves into—the "ropers," the "socials," the "nerds," the "jocks," and so on, ad infinitum.

In fact, a good CARE Team leader realizes that the more recalcitrant and authority-hating the sub-demographic—the "dopers" or the "outsiders"—the more heavily she should attempt to recruit from their ranks, because these are where the most problems may exist.

The major role of the CARE teams is to reach out to troubled students before their problems overwhelm them. Those problems can range from soured relationships to tangles with parents to holiday blues.

When the CARE teams began forming, the reaction of other students slowly changed from one of bemusement to that of grudging acceptance. At first it was as if people were thinking, "Don't talk to me, I'm fine. I'm not going to kill myself."

But then came James Austin Stailey.

Things changed the day he walked up to the lectern in his Arlington High School drama class.

It was January 19, 1985.

Stailey was a quiet boy who liked to listen to Beethoven, read science fiction and fantasy novels, and dream of being a great stage director. In fact, the night before he walked up to that lectern, he'd played the lead role in an Arlington High School production of the Tom Stoppard play, *The Real Inspector Hound*. It was his second part in a school play, and he had told his sister he was going to be able to direct the next one in March. Stailey, though shy, was well-liked, and had a philosophical bent.

All his friends would come over to his house and sit up until dawn and talk about philosophy and the theory of relativity and whether or not time exists—that was one of his favorite questions—and try to dispute some of Newton's laws of motion.

But beyond his drama activities, Stailey was not a joiner at school. He didn't like group sports like baseball or football. He was into Kung Fu, but mostly for philosophical reasons, liking the mental discipline and the soul-searching.

Then, that morning, standing at the lectern, he talked a lot about life's meaning, and how unhappy he was with what he saw around him in life. Violence in particular bothered him, and it frustrated him that people couldn't learn to get along. He imagined the world could be so much better, but he said no one else could understand that. He went on like this for some little while, and finally, one of the kids in the group asked (rhetorically, the poor kid believed): "If it's so bad, why don't you kill yourself?"

"Good idea," said Stailey, and he casually pulled a sawed-off shotgun out of his leather briefcase and shot himself in the head.

The class went into shock. And then the school. And then the community.

But there was a difference this time.

We were, of course, all dazed.

I had been at home for lunch when I got the call. All the dispatcher knew for certain was that there had been a shooting at Arlington High School and one student was believed to be dead. "The info is that he shot himself," I was told.

I went to the school and was met by some school officials. As they were taking me through the crowd of kids, there was the constant chatter of, "Did you hear? Someone got shot."

As we got closer to the room where he'd done it, the content of the chatter changed to "Did you hear that somebody killed himself? Do you know who it was???"

And, past the police line, in what should have remained just an ordinary classroom, there he lay, in a pool of blood, shattered, gone forever.

And, in his own way, he was talking.

The dead do talk, you know—and none are more talkative than suicides. A lot of times they don't know the *first thing* about what they are talking about; they are frequently tremendous founts of misinformation. But they are talking nonetheless—almost jabbering, in fact, once you learn to listen. Sometimes, they are talking about their lives. Sometimes, they are talking about their misconceptions about death. And sometimes, sadder and more ironic still, there are those cases where the statement they are trying to make with their death is completely at odds with the one the listeners get.

Of course, sometimes I just plain don't hear them right. Something gets lost in the translation. Suicide is not an easy language. Sometimes it's just a look on that dead face, or the reactions of the survivors. Sometimes the words come from the circumstances surrounding the death, which are often subtle and difficult to divine.

I only half-remember the interview that followed Stailey's death with Dave Tarrant of the *Dallas Morning News*.

"You always wonder what you could have done that you didn't do," I told him. "You have the feeling that, had we been aware or had we been alert, we could have seen this coming. But most of us are not aware of every action of a friend or a relative."

The family was at a complete loss. His sister, Julia, said that if she'd had the remotest clue that James was going to do what he did, she would have gathered everyone who cared for him into one room, just to tell him they loved him. A few days after his death, Julia displayed two sheets of yellow legal paper with writing on them. "This is something I never showed him," she said at the time. "I think maybe if he knew someone else thought things like this, he would have hesitated."

It was a poem she'd written quite some time before he died. It read:

There comes a time when all hope dies
And emotions lose all hold

When tomorrow's dream has slipped away
And memories fade to gold.
And though the clues be strewn about,
The answer isn't there.
The silent screams and pleas for help
Fall upon thin air.

And she said, "I was thinking this morning about the whole teenage suicide problem—all the kids out there who thought they were alone in their unhappiness. I hope my brother wasn't too alone."

One of the most pressing questions for his friends on that Saturday was why he had chosen to do it at school. I told a reporter at the time that I thought it was in order to say to his family, "You're not to blame." With hindsight, though, I think it was to say, "Watch *this!*"

Almost all suicides, and potential suicides who change their minds and live—and it is from them that we know this—engage in some kind of after-life fantasy, particularly concerning where they'll be and what they'll be doing during the funeral. These little fantasies are almost always simplistic. "Mother will be sad" or "Daddy will be sorry" is actually a far cry from all the other things those people will be feeling as the conflicting emotions that come in the wake of a suicide begin. Mother will also be mad, and Daddy may also be very disgusted. But the common denominator of all of these is that the victim assumes he, too, will be there, if not somewhere even better.

Over the years I've come to know that, in order for someone to commit suicide, at least two conditions must be met. First, there must be pain—physical, or, more often, mental. And second, there must be in the victim's mind a view that death is somehow benign, a state worth working toward—a state which the victim will be there, somehow, to enjoy. They may picture it as oblivion—but an oblivion they will somehow "live" to enjoy.

For suicide to occur, the pain must be sufficient to overcome any potential negative perceptions of death. That is, it takes less pain to produce suicide in someone who has positive expectations of death.

I believe that James Austin Stailey may have had some of the pain. But I think that in his case, it was his notion of death that seduced him, that allowed him to let the pain push him to pull that trigger.

The CARE teams and other efforts around the country are there to intervene with the pain. Maybe Stailey couldn't reach out, or maybe people didn't hear him reaching out. One teacher at the school told his students after the shooting that Stailey had talked to him after class the day before about suicide. The teacher told the class he hadn't thought it significant until after he heard the news of Stailey's death. And a friend told classmates that Stailey had questioned him Friday morning in the lunchroom about the meaning of life. That, too, had not seemed particularly significant.

After Stailey's death, we found we had done some things right. When the two boys had been found dead in the pickup two years earlier, mass confusion had reigned. After Stailey's death, however, students, school officials, parents, and community health professionals all began drawing together for answers and support. Officials in various programs were able to offer more information about suicide prevention to all Arlington High students and to provide individual counseling for the students and a teacher who had been with Stailey when he shot himself.

"It's not a setback, but a test of what we've put together so far," Velma Bogart, one of the CARE program's founders, said at the time.

We'd passed. We hadn't saved James Stailey, but we were solidly in place to help the surviving students.

The most important thing to us was that in the wake of Stailey's death no "cluster" effect would follow. None did. And, though it sounds insensitive, in the long-term, student acceptance and awareness of the CARE groups greatly increased after Stailey's death. Nonetheless, everybody connected with the CARE teams—including me—did a lot of soul-searching.

One of the things I realized was that, by the very

nature of my job as chaplain to the Arlington Police Department, I was in a reactive position most of the time. When asked to counsel those in pain, I counseled. But most of my day-to-day activities were focused on meeting the emotional needs of the police department, not the community at large. Then I realized that there might be a way to expand my usefulness; to correct misconceptions by setting out to tell the plain truth about suicide rather than simply fighting the pain through counseling.

I see it over and over again, and so I'll say it over and over again.

Suicide *is not* painless. Suicide *is not* painless. *Suicide is not painless.*

Chapter 4

We can't really imagine what death is like. On the other hand, we can ONLY imagine what death is like.

We've said that, for someone to commit suicide, there must be pain—physical, or, more often, mental. To hope to intervene is not impossible—but it's tricky, since first you must *identify* the individual, who may not want to be identified (or know that he wants to be identified). Then you must establish communication, often against resistance. And then you must help deal with the pain.

Second, there must be in the victim's mind some view that death is benign, a state worth working toward—a state in which the victim believes he will be, and will somehow enjoy the peace he believes death holds. He may vaguely picture it as oblivion—but an oblivion he will somehow "live" to enjoy.

It has been said that it is impossible for us to imagine our individual extinction. I believe that in order for suicide to occur, the pain the person is enduring must be sufficient to overcome any potential negative perceptions of death. (In other words, it takes less pain to produce suicide in someone who has positive expectations of death.)

I believe that James Austin Stailey may have had some of the former—the pain. But I think that in his case, it was the latter that seduced him, that allowed him to let the pain push him to pull that trigger. And the pulling of the trigger was James Austin Stailey's choice; in fact, it's every suicide's choice. But it's a decision that can't be undone because no other choices follow.

But positive expectations of death are partly our responsibility as a culture, and also something we may have some little control over. Here is where, as a society, we may intervene in a general sense.

In cases where I have worked a suicide, the family of the victim, not having a church of their own, will ask me to "preach the funeral." That, to me, is a sad sign of the times—that people are so disjointed and divorced from a supportive community that they should have to ask the man who has just said "I'm sorry, your son is dead," to preach at the boy's funeral.

My sadness for them makes this request impossible to refuse. Many times they have no one else to turn to, and I've said my fair share of elegies. And, both before and after, if it is an open-coffin service, it is not unusual for someone to say, "Oh, Chaplain Elliott, it looks like he's only sleeping, doesn't it?"

And of course I say, "Oh yes, it does, yes, only sleeping."

Because that is the right thing to say to them.

But it is NOT the right thing to say to the world at large, and to others who might be tempted to follow the example. Nevertheless, we keep on saying it.

In fact, as a culture, we insist on saying it: "Death, where is thy sting?" And, "It's beautiful upon that farther shore." And, "He's happier now." And... so on.

Over the course of human history we have been working hard at getting everyone to agree that death isn't bad. Death's OK. Let's not worry about death, all right? And that has been, for the most part, a good thing. Too obsessive a fear of death would, at worst, make you want to kill yourself just to get it over with.

For the still-healthy (and subjectively, if you're like me, thus eternal), our perceptions of the major afflictions—and endings—are based on external appearances. We cringe at the thought of burning alive, even though a much more likely demise by, say, cancer, with no horrible external damage to make onlookers wince, may be subjectively worse by far.

And thus it is with death.

We think of Death not in terms of how it actually is—authoritative first-hand reporting being somewhat scant—but in terms of how it looks.

In the Dark and the Middle Ages, people would carry with them "mementos mori," reminders of death—a bit of bone, perhaps—to remind them that life was transitory. But they really needed no reminders. Life then was nasty, brutish, and short. But as people of the times could plainly see, and smell, it beat the alternative.

Death—and the ghastly stench and the grisly sight of death, of liquefying flesh—was everywhere, and never far from your front door. It got your neighbor one day and might come knocking for you the next, or a plague might just take everyone on the block. A man who lived to forty was hoary with great age.

The early Christians had, during the years of their suppression by the Romans, used catacombs as mass graves for their dead. Even after their suffrage, the practice of burying the dead in uncomfortably close proximity to the living continued—in the courtyards and vaults of churches.

By as early as the sixth century, burial vaults in churches were crowded with rotted coffins. In warm months the air crackled and buzzed with stench and flies. The scene outdoors in many churchyards was worse—and it was a scene that most people were required by both law and custom to see at least once a week.

Coffins would have been stacked in the ground until, in many cases, the most recent additions were only an inch or two from the ground's surface. When the stacks began to rise above the natural level of the ground, the ground was raised until it reached the church windows.

By the onset of the Renaissance and until the early part of the nineteenth century, despite other human advances, Death remained visible in the graveyards of most cities and towns. To make room for the unending supply of fresh corpses, church sextons would surreptitiously discharge the older corpses to secret pits or to stacks of bones in charnel houses, and then secretly sell the coffin's metal fittings as scrap.

In America through the Colonial years and the early

years of the Union, the situation was no better. And the interment problems brought on by increasing urbanization in the more crowded Northeast rivaled those in Europe.

As a series of epidemics of yellow fever and other diseases raced through their populace in the early eighteen hundreds, Eastern cities were literally swamped with dead, whose numbers were turning the earth into quagmires. Philadelphia used city-owned vacant lots to bury the dead, and sites where children were at play one day were covered in tombstones and crucifixes the next day. Boston's City Council called for the immediate cessation of all burials within the city limits as well as the exhumation of all shallow graves.

In 1820 a travel writer touring America wrote of a relatively underpopulated Eastern Seaboard graveyard: "A soppy churchyard, where the mourners sink ankle deep in a rank and offensive mold, mixed with broken bones and fragments of coffins."

Then, in the summer of 1822, the city of New York was hit by an epidemic of yellow fever that left sixteen thousand dead—and a need for as many brand-new graves.

Even in the mostly unpopulated portions of the American frontier in the eighteen hundreds, graveyards were forlorn and forbidding patches, vine-shrouded and overgrown with brambles. For the most part they were avoided, since no one needed a reminder of a brief life's inevitable and always premature end.

But thanks at least in part to a healthy reaction to disease, Death was about to get a physical make-over that would make him much more appealing. And thanks to a new school of poets, he was about to become very much en vogue, with his gloom reconstituted as glory.

Up until this time, literature (and thus the cultural consciousness) on the subject of death and suicide had pretty much followed the masses' perceptions and, to a lesser extent, the orthodoxies of the church. And the church's proscriptions against suicide were stiff. Early on, the church even had a problem with "martyrs" taking the quick way to Heaven by being rather unreasonably cooperative with those who would slay them. The church had come down hard on such people. By the Middle Ages, suicide was, in the eyes of the church, such a horror that disfigurements and outrages against the corpses of those who tried it were carried out with all the solemnity the priests could muster. The masses stood by as corpses were dragged through the streets.

And the poets were on hand to savage them in print.

Writing at the start of the thirteen hundreds, Dante devoted one of the harshest cantatas of his *Inferno* to suicides, assigning them to the Seventh Circle, below even the heretics and the murderers simmering in hot blood.

The day-to-day folk took a dim view of Death, and evidenced a morbid and fearful preoccupation with all the grim physical details, the worms and decay, the brief nature of life, and with God's allegedly ruthless judgment.

Throughout the Middle Ages the commonest depiction in woodcuts, paintings and tapestries was the familiar Dance of Death, wherein a happy-go-lucky grinning skeleton escorts away the frightened living, kings and commoners alike. As one writer well put it, "Death was the one form of political equality the Middle Ages understood, an equality of terror..."

It may be that there is a corollary between a culture's views on Death and Death's actual proximity. When it is closest it is naturally most feared and shunned. Conversely, when life is easiest, death is perceived as being more user-friendly.

By the time of the Renaissance, living conditions—as compared to the grim, hardscrabble, lice-ridden and plague-ridden daily horror of feudal times—had improved to the extent that there was a growing class of free-thinking scholars with the latitude, education and discretion to rediscover and study the classics of Rome and Greece. (These had themselves been produced in a more expansive age and in a time when suicide was not much reviled.) Francis Bacon and other Renaissance writers took an increasingly lenient view of both death and suicide, holding that the only thing that mattered was the dignity and stylishness brought to the act. But fourteen of Shakespeare's characters elected to kill themselves rather than live through the rest of the play, and many of the ones who did stay with the script spent a deal of time pondering whether to be or not to be.

There was still a certain duality between fiction and real life.

Romeo and Juliet's suicide in the play was seen as beautiful and ennobling by the audience, but, had these teens tried it offstage, the audience might still have tied them to a horse and dragged them through the streets to be dumped into an unmarked grave. However, Shakespeare was far from alone in his straightforward sentiments on suicide.

In 1608, John Donne wrote his *Biathanatos*: A Declaration of that... Thesis, "That Self-homicide is not so naturally Sinne, that it may never be otherwise." (He later thought better of it, asking friends and family, upon his demise, not to allow it to be published.) This marked yet a further stage in literature's depiction—and thus, society's perceptions—of suicide. Where Shakespeare's suicides had quitted themselves for reasons of stoic nobility, John Donne was literarily kicking around the notion that one might do it on grounds of merely being in a terrible mood. That Donne was in such a mood—and a chronic one, perhaps indicative of the clinical depression he was experiencing at the time he wrote it—became clear in a letter he wrote to a friend that same year, 1608. The letter also makes clear that, were it not for his personal adherence to the very same religious proscriptions against suicide that his *Biathanatos* argues against, John Donne might indeed have killed himself.

"...I have often suspected myself to be overtaken... with a desire of the next life: which though I know it is not merely out of weariness in this, because I had the same desires when (times were good), and enjoyed fairer hopes than now: yet I doubt worldly encombrances have encreased it. I would not that death should take me asleep... but win me, and overcome me... therefore I would fain DO something... for to this hour I am nothing, or so little, that I am scarce subject and argument good enough for one of mine own letters..."

In addition to the great literary influence of the outrageous love poetry written in his youth, John Donne went on to become the most renowned and seductive preacher of his day, But at the time he penned *Biathanatos*, he was in the doldrums, way down in the dark valley between these two professional and personal peaks. Donne's writing may have been an attempt at catharsis—of getting rid of depression by putting it on paper. The mental exercise of writing it and arguing it well may have restored some of his self-esteem and confidence in his old abilities, and in his faith that these would one day again prevail.

Were it not for Donne's poetry, his lovely but dark yearnings toward death might not have colored the cultural mind. His "A Nocturnall upon S. Lucies Day, Being the Shortest Day," was written probably sometime after 1607—and, from the tone, in the short-lived light of a particularly dark and dreary December 21 at that. It is great poetry. Great dreary poetry. For the impressionable, perhaps, great and deadly poetry.

A new breeze was rustling the leaves of literature and carrying a strangely sweetened smell of Death. By the nineteenth century, that breeze would have become a gale—one that would blow down countless lives.

Chapter 5

If the romanticizing of suicide by the romantic poets can be traced to any one event, it is the suicide of poet Thomas Chatterton. Within a generation of his death he would become the supreme symbol of the sensitive but proud, brilliant but misunderstood, soft-hearted but fearless, poet.

The funny thing about Chatterton is that he killed himself not out of any vast sensitivity or poetic impulse, but out of vain and bullish pride: He was determined that if he could not make a living as a writer (rather than in the menial tasks generally assigned the class in which he was born), he just wasn't going to go on living at all. The rigidity of the British caste system at the time is what led him to do himself in; the snobs simply wouldn't let him up.

By the time he was seventeen, and had graduated from charity school and been apprenticed to a scrivener, he had invented a remarkable literary playmate named Thomas Rowley, a prolific fifteenth century poet-monk, whose manuscripts were claimed to have been found at St. Mary Redcliffe. Chatterton had—in an extraordinary display of literary precocity—written these himself on parchment in a highly believable medieval style. It did him little good. Three of Bristol's leading lights relieved him of many of the "Rowley" manuscripts for a few shillings.

He compounded the misfortune of low birth by trying to enlist the support of a truly lousy patron. Horace Walpole was one of the literary lions of the age, rich, well-connected and influential. Chatterton would learn that he was also self-absorbed, vain, stingy, and a hopeless snob—the last person in the world who would help some promising but low-born young man.

Chatterton sent him one of "Rowley's" best, an elaborate work of bogus scholarship. Walpole was taken in, excited to be part of the "discovery" of Rowley, and wrote Chatterton suggesting he might be interested in publishing the Rowley poems. Chatterton made the mistake of believing that Walpole liked the work itself, rather than the opportunity for snobbish posing that such a discovery afforded. He revealed both his own poverty-stricken background and the fact that he was actually a poor poet in search of a patron. Walpole dropped Chatterton flat, informing him that poetry was a pursuit for gentlemen.

The vast talent, the incredible ear for language, the cleverness, and the ingenuity with which Chatterton wrote was not enough to overcome his low birth. He continued to work for the scrivener for only his keep, no wages. He had to eat with the servants and share a bedroom with the footman, and his pride, which had swelled on his initial good fortune with Walpole, now chafed at his dim prospects.

Some of his pride came from his handsomeness and personal magnetism; he had an undeniably regal presence, not because of artifice or pose, but because of an unbankable fire within. It was hard for him to subvert this into the kind of scraping subservience expected from one of his class. Although of poor family, he was the only boy, and had been spoiled, a poor preparation for his life and station. Though his poems started appearing in magazines, he was not recompensed, and his debts began to become insurmountable.

He wrote a suicide note which he left in full view. His master found it and persuaded friend William Barrett to intervene.

As Chatterton explained to Barrett:

"It is my PRIDE, my damn'd, native, unconquerable Pride, that plunges me into distraction. You must know that 19/20 of my Composition is Pride. I must either live a Slave, a Servant; to have no Will of my own, no Sentiments of my own which I may freely declare as such;—or DIE—perplexing alternative!"

Soon, after more difficulties with money and patronage, he wrote yet another suicide note forecasting his demise for the following evening—and once again left the letter lying around, where it was soon again discovered by his master, John Lambert. Lambert, disturbed by the prospect of a suicide in his home, released Chatterton immediately from the indentures which bound him.

A week later, Chatterton left for London, convinced that he could make his way there as a writer. His confidence seemed well-founded; he had already been published in city magazines and the editors had been encouraging, if vague. Once he was in town, they too were impressed with his personal presence, accepting his manuscripts and making even bigger promises than before. Soon his satiric verse and political essays were being prolifically published—and systematically exploited. When the editors paid him at all, they grossly underpaid him. Then, two of the editors who were chief among his supporters were imprisoned for political reasons. Those remaining outside the Old Bailey began avoiding Chatterton and his political tirades like the plague.

He had almost hit bottom when his luck once again turned for the better. He had written a letter in favor of William Beckford, Lord Mayor; the mayor approved of the piece and wanted another written about him. Chatterton persuaded William Bingley to publish it in the *North Briton*, then the most prestigious of London's weeklies. Bingley agreed to even more—to devote a whole issue of the paper to Chatterton's prose! The article was already set in print when Beckford caught a cold and died.

By then, most of London's cosmopolites were leaving for the country for the summer. There was no one to sell anything to because there was nobody left in town.

For a while, Chatterton gave himself over to his rage and hurt—then once again began trying to pick up the pieces. More rotten luck followed. He'd picked up enough of the basics of medicine from his friend Barrett that, given the knowledge of the times, would have qualified him to serve as a ship's doctor—provided that Barrett would so certify; but Barrett did not. None of the editors who owed him money were paying him. He had no money, so, soon, he was not eating.

On August 24, his landlady, knowing he had not eaten for at least two days, begged him to have dinner with her. She reported that Chatterton was offended at the request as it hinted that he was "in want."

Neighbors heard him pacing restlessly far into the night. He failed to appear the next morning and by afternoon they forced his door, finding "a horrid spectacle, with features distorted, as if from convulsions."

Thomas Chatterton, three months shy of his eighteenth birthday, had taken arsenic.

No one claimed his body.

And then he received a final slight: In the Register of Deaths, they got his name wrong, recording him as "William" Chatterton.

His reasons for suicide? To take life and "fling it away like a flower," in James' words, and thus expiate his failure? Perhaps. But it was also the looming prospect of starvation, a run of bad luck, and a deadly mixture of vanity and stubbornness disguised as noble pride. Thanks to Chatterton and his lionizers (who, because they, too, were poets, were actually congratulating themselves on their own noble suffering), youth and poetry and death became synonymous.

The great difference between the Romantic revolution and the Renaissance was the way in which the Romantics made literature not an accessory but a necessity, a way of life.

Four years after Chatterton's death, Goethe's *The Sorrows of Young Werther* was published. This literary suicide exemplified unrequited love and excessive sensibility, and led to countless real suicides by young Europeans who shared his traits—or wished to believe they did. They proved it by "joining" him in an epidemic of self-slaughter that continued for decades throughout Europe. Since authors were the rock stars of the day, the public took a very personal and proprietary attitude toward them and their characters.

The word "genius" had once been reserved for those who had in some precocious and productive way distinguished themselves; now it became a sobriquet claimed by young men who were merely bizarre, willful, and moody.

These poor gifted boys, these poets. Had they lived longer, more mature work might have supplanted what was at least in some part the gloomy posturings of youths who suddenly found their scribblings in vogue. But Keats died of tuberculosis at age twenty-six, Shelley drowned at twenty-nine, and Lord Byron died of malaria at the ripe old age of thirty-six.

A strange reverberation from the Romantic revolution, and one still echoing loudly in our own time, persisted through the years. The Romantic literati embraced the notion that any poet who lived into middle age ought to be ashamed, because he'd surely lost his spark. The sad thing is that this shaky assertion took hold. Chatterton's tough life and youthful suicide would thus become the foundation for one of our most seductive archetypes: The Lonely Misunderstood Genius Who Just May Be Too Sensitive and Brilliant to Live This Tawdry Life In A Cold and Futile World.

Particularly for young people, there's a great insidious allure to this.

First, it elevates mere unhappiness to the higher, nobler status of suffering. No young person is comfortable living with a strong conviction that they might just be undeniably average and indistinguishable from anybody else. It takes years to accept that.

Second, it enables us to deny that we might not be perfect by placing blame on others and the world. It provides an instant and ennobling excuse for just about every possible negative observation that can be made about the person who has embraced that designation. Average grades? Average looks? Haven't done anything to distinguish yourself? Well, it's hard, when you're a lonely, misunderstood genius in a cold and futile world. I mean, like, why TRY?

The insidiousness and the allure lies partly in its self-reinforcing nature. Every slight, every failure buttresses this. It might be relatively harmless if it simply allowed the as-yet-undistinguished to live comfortably within themselves until such time as they could indeed produce something earth-shattering—or learn to face the fact that most of us *are* pretty average.

But there is a price tag. He who is misunderstood cannot help but feel isolated. He who is isolated can't help but feel sullen. He who is sullen is not much fun to be around. So he is further isolated, and further misunderstood, and sullen...

And before long everybody's pretty sick of you and wouldn't voluntarily give you the time of day, much less help you with anything you cared about—so now it IS a cold and futile world, because you're getting the cold and futile shoulder.

I have reason to suspect that James Stailey was a victim—a believer in that cold and futile world.

I wonder whether his choice of literary company—or his taking their statements too seriously—might have had something to do with where he is now.

Thomas Chatterton swallowed that arsenic more than two hundred years ago. But the poison keeps on killing. I can't prove it, of course—but I believe it killed James Austin Stailey, and may kill a lot more like him, before it's run its course.

And the only thing we can do is put it into perspective.

Chapter 6

It had taken little more than a generation for death to make the transition from dreaded Dark Horseman to a sort of dreary Dear Heart, a wistful Welcome Wagon worker dispensing sweet melancholy to all who arrived on the far shore.

Death, as the eighteen hundreds marched on, now meant "deliverance from this mundane world, a glorious reunion with loved ones in the palace of heaven." Even the great plague of the period, tuberculosis, was getting the red-carpet welcome from writers of the time. In *David Copperfield*, Dickens found it profitable to let Little Blossom gracefully fade from consumption, and the very willows wept. It was a beautiful way to die.

Alexander Dumas had his lady of the camellias pass from this vale with but one delicate cough—which cough Puccini made even more melancholically beautiful, setting it to music in *La Traviata*.

Under these perverse circumstances, it was only natural that death no longer be assigned to the grimness of the churchyard and the charnel house. The general feeling was that a lavish death style was desirable. Thus, the garden cemetery movement was born, and death had never looked so good.

New England botanist and physician Dr. Jacob Bigelow had two great loves: Cemetery reform and horticulture, and he married these two in his dream of a garden cemetery. As a physician, he saw that it would mean the end of the festering miasmic messes in the churchyards and the disease they spread. As a botanist, he saw it as a place where nature could be recruited to provide the scenery.

In August 1831, the botany fans and the reformers were able to round up one hundred wealthy Bostonians who were worried about their own last addresses, and with contributions of six thousand dollars, the land became Mt. Auburn, a model for the garden cemetery movement and the modern municipal park. Thus quietly began a movement that would transform the face of death itself.

The press was on hand to praise Mt. Auburn's sylvan scenery as a "place of succor," teaching the living a lesson in "natural theology." And a review in the *New England Magazine* lectured, "In the mighty system of the universe not a single step of the destroyer, Time, but is subservient to some ulterior purpose of reproduction... the circle of creation and destruction is eternal."

People were dying to get in: The rich paid for their plots, but the poor were permitted to barter. Small businessmen and bookkeepers swapped their ledger-domain for plots, and farmers plowed trails in exchange for family graves.

And the living were dying to get in, too, for recreation. Boston's space-starved urban populace came to Mt. Auburn for picnics and weekend outings by the thousands; where once the dominions of death were to be avoided, now they were vacation spots.

Death was looking better all the time—so good, in fact, that these words, penned by a reporter after the opening of Green-Wood Cemetery in New York in 1838, may have even more relevance for citizens of the late twentieth century:

"Ever since he entered these greenwood shades, he has been sensibly getting farther and farther from strife, and business, and care... a short half-hour ago, he was in the midst of a discordant Babel; he was one of the hurrying, jostling crowd; he was encompassed by the whirl and fever of artificial life. Now he stands alone in Nature's inner court—in her silent, solemn sanctuary. Her holiest influences are all around him."

Across the country, bereavement was being stealthily

encircled and surrounded by beauty, and the focus of the living turned slowly from the deceased to the setting of the burial.

The literature being handed out by supporters of the garden cemeteries promoted three themes of reunion, aimed at easing the separation that death threatened. At death, said they, the deceased individual could expect to commune with God, with nature, and with deceased family and friends.

From here on out, the "dying" of death increased at a dramatic rate.

"Today cemetery-making is an art," said one writer, "and gradually all things that suggest death, sorrow, or pain, are being eliminated." First to go were the fences that had theretofore enclosed individual graves and family plots. Next went another unsightly reminder of death—the grave mound; then the last long-term reminder of death, the tombstone.

Beyond the aesthetics, and their detraction from the park-like effect, tombstones represented "sentiment" and "tradition" in a now enlightened age. Big monuments were decried.

Death, as an enemy, died. Where once the graveyards indicated death and decay, the cemeteries now shouted resurrection and life. Where once the fetid air drove men out, now the aroma of flowers drew them in. Where once it was a place you had to go sooner or later, now it was somewhere you could look forward to going—a place where you could finally get to spend some quality time.

In 1901, an ad for a Brooklyn cemetery summed it all up rather well:

"Graves finely situated, surrounded by the beauties of nature, commanding a fine view of the bay, and, in short, meeting with every requirement of the human family. People who have tried them cannot be persuaded to go elsewhere."

As the garden-cemetery movement grew (by 1861 there were sixty-seven of them in the United States), America began to perceive that cemeteries were nice places to be.

The only perceptual deterrent remaining was the fact that the natural decaying processes began the moment life fled, and so the deceased himself usually looked pretty bad by the time he got there. The grieving family itself usually handled the arrangements. The female members of the family prepared the body for burial, placing it on a board between two chairs and washing it. (In warm weather, they put a large chunk of ice (if they had it) in a tub beneath the board, with smaller chunks about the body.) Then they dressed the body for burial in a simple shroud or winding sheet. Usually little more than two days elapsed from the time of death to the time of interment, to allow close kin to come from distances to pay their respects. And they usually made haste, for it was always a race against time. It was, in other words, death in the raw. Not the kind you find in funeral homes. Not the kind you find in hospitals. It was death—raw, rigor-mortised, cold, close, and clammy.

But over the course of the nineteenth century, as both the poets and the horticulturist reformers made the final destination more agreeable as an end, undertakers began to make the journey there easier upon the survivors. The changes came gradually.

At first the undertaker was the one who made you a simple wooden coffin, which you then took home, and put your deceased in. Then you hauled it out to the graveyard (and a little later, to the garden cemetery), where you and your friends and family buried it.

Then the undertaker began to come to your house and prepare the body himself. Then he added a small stock of ready-made coffins and some other trimmings. Then he added a special box to his wagon to make it a hearse so he could do the hauling for you.

But it was the Civil War that really expanded the business of death, with the advent of modern embalming. (Modern embalming differs from the ancient kind used by the Egyptians. The modern practice is to remove all blood from the veins and arteries and replace it with preserving chemicals. William Harvey had thought of it in the sixteen hundreds, after his discovery of the circulatory network, but it did not become widespread for centuries, since it was considered too grisly and disrespectful of the deceased.)

Then, five years before the Civil War, J. Anthony Gaussardia, a Washington entrepreneur, had the good fortune to patent this process. When the Civil War was underway and Union troops were dying by the thousands, embalming allowed them to be preserved for the long, slow train ride home.

What really sold America on the benefits of embalming was a tour of Abraham Lincoln's body. After his preserved corpse was viewed by thousands of people in Washington, millions more eyed his enduring remains at train depots along his route to his first and final home—Springfield, Illinois.

And so embalming soon formed the very cornerstone of the mortuary business.

Americans were now seeing beyond preserving corpses merely for transport. They believed that, since the body was the temple of the Holy Spirit, embalming showed respect. And embalmers began to make those who had died look as if they hadn't. By maintaining the lifelike appearance of a corpse so that it would look "natural," embalmers succeeded in directing attention from the fact that the natural appearance of a body is in no way lifelike.

Next to go was the time-honored habit of dressing as if one were dead. Gone were the sepulchral shrouds and winding sheet. Now the dead were dressed in their finest, and funeral directors began to refer to their clients as "only sleeping."

Thus by the use of chemicals, cosmetics, and words, embalmers/undertakers blurred the difference between life and death, narrowing the chasm between both states. And the narrower people believe that chasm to be, the more similar they believe one side is to the other, the easier it is to jump.

I see the jumpers. And every so often, I encounter a case that proves all too graphically the narrowness of this gap.

Every so often, I get someone who has bought into the appearances. He will come out to the cemetery in his car. He will park not too far away from the main building of the funeral home. He will, usually either by asphyxiation or by gunshot, kill himself.

And we will find a note on the decedent's person suggesting that (1) he doesn't want to be any trouble and (2) the reason he chose this locale was so that he would be convenient for all concerned. That someone from the funeral home could just come on out and get him, take him inside, pop him in the box, have someone say a few words over him, and then take him to his underground bungalow on Swan Avenue in the Garden o' Memories, where he can just sit out eternity listening to the birds sing and watching the grass grow and the seasons come and go.

It's all a matter of perspective.

Chapter 7

And now, back to the real world, where life is hard and death isn't pretty and people have enough serious problems and wrong solutions that they can be lured from one to the other—from a hard life to an unlovely death.

Obviously, not everyone who drinks and has a bad relationship is going to kill themselves. But sometimes it seems to me that those who kills themselves have had a drink, or a bad relationship, or both.

Objectively, I know that I have worked some, perhaps even many, where neither were a factor. But if I were a betting man, and you told me that Joe Doakes committed suicide, I'd bet on alcohol and a broken relationship.

Again and again, scene after scene.

Sitting here in my office, I can pick up my notebooks, open them to any page...

Al Jones, twenty-five. He'd had considerable problems with alcohol, and thus with holding jobs or staying in school. His dad came by to wake him up and found him lying in the floor in the middle of food wrappers and beer cans. At that point, late in the morning, Al was still alive. He got the boy up. Came back later to check on him and the door was locked. Dad knocked on the door, then went around to sliding glass door and entered the apartment. Al had crawled into the bathtub and shot himself. He left an illegible note.

Joe F., attorney. He had some alcohol problems and marital problems, plus financial problems, so he went in and sat down on the couch of his comfortable home and put a bullet in his brain.

Dan M., twenty-one. He'd been in rehab for alcohol.

After he got out, everybody thought he was doing all right. Living at home, he picked up his parents at the airport after their trip out of town. Everything seemed normal. About midnight, he said he was going to go out and wax his car. They found him the next morning, lying under the exhaust pipe of the car, his head on a pillow. An ice chest in the back seat held three or four empty beer cans.

Then there was John Ruff, fifty-six, who shot his live-in girlfriend, Sue, sixty-five, as she slept. Then he turned the gun on himself. He was an alcoholic, and was to have been committed that day.

Just flipping through the pages, on and on and... the phone rings.

It's the dispatcher. Someone has killed himself.

You won't read about it in the newspaper. Because there's so much of it that it isn't news.

The dispatcher said there have been two suicides in twenty-four hours, not all that unusual. The one last night was a fifty-four-year-old schizophrenic, and disabled. He'd been drinking. Shot himself right in front of his wife. She seemed like a really nice person. She had some disabilities of her own, but had been able to keep working. But they'd had a misunderstanding. She said she was leaving to do some errands. All he heard was "leaving." She couldn't convince him otherwise. It was a pretty big misunderstanding.

Mental illness frequently enters into it. (In fact, one Christmas Day a forty-five-year-old schizophrenic and manic-depressive who lived with his mother came downstairs, told her he hadn't slept well and that he was going to go upstairs and take a nap. Since it was Christmas, his sister had come over and when the table was all set, she went upstairs and knocked on the door. When he didn't open it, she did. The covers were pulled up above his head, so she pulled them back. He was dead.)

Now, on the way to this scene, I realize yet again: There is almost nowhere I can go in this town without passing an old suicide scene that sends my memory back to sad lives ending on sadder notes—to me, the saddest possible note, because none of them had to end that way. And this town is no better or worse than most, when it comes to suicide.

There, that motel. The Val-U Inn.

A young man had just left Wichita State Hospital, and he had three or four bottles of pills and two gallons of booze. He took them to the room along with a brand new shotgun, not even out of the box, just in case the other stuff didn't do the trick. But the pills got him. He lay dead in that room for a week before they smelled him.

Lots of folks go to seedy motels to do it, figuring that at least someone will find them by the next day.

And those apartments?

Those apartments there, second floor. A young man hanged himself from a ceiling fan. It was really pretty rough. He'd called his ex-girlfriend and said, "If you don't come back to me, I'm going to kill myself." She told him she wasn't coming back.

He said, "OK," and the next thing she heard, over the phone, was gurgling. He'd stepped off the stool, phone in hand—and he held onto the receiver until he lost consciousness.

There are so many of them that sometimes when I'm tired I can't get them all sorted out in my mind. Most days I don't want to know more about them than I have to.

How'd they look? How'd they do it? Who do I have to notify?

I look, I listen, I go. I always carry horrible news.

This one today is typical—if that adjective can be applied to an event of such magnitude as suicide.

It's a fairly nice house, sort of a high-end "starter home." A thirty-eight-year-old part-time machine tools sales manager and full-time alcoholic is in the living room. It looks as if he'd done some work on the ceiling, because there is a hole in the sheet rock, exposing a rafter. Tied around the rafter is a yellow nylon rope. The other end of the rope is tied around his neck.

When people hang themselves, you usually find them dangling, their feet a foot off the floor. Most hangings are actually self-strangulations. In this case, he had sat in a chair and leaned forward, choking himself. He was lying almost prone on the floor, face down, his head maybe six inches above the beige carpet—although during the night the rope may have stretched a bit.

He was separated from his wife and had been missing from work for a day or two. The secretary from his office had gone over the preceding night to check on him because he didn't answer the phone. Nobody had answered the door. She had called his mother this morning. His mother didn't know anything, so she had called the police.

And so here he is. The wax mannequin syndrome is something the bodies always help you with—by not moving, even though in the back of your mind you always half expect them to. As always, the crime scene officers turn him over so I can check his face, because that is the first thing the relatives will want to know. It is purple and swollen, but nothing that can't be fixed. Fixed cosmetically, anyway.

The crime scene officers are routinely scratching and scraping around the premises for any evidence that might indicate a possible homicide—but it doesn't take a rocket scientist to tell what this was. The officers do not require me, at least, not in the counseling sense.

That is not always the case.

The medical examiner's field agent is on the way. He'll poke and prod some too, and then take him on down to the morgue, where they'll perform an autopsy. In most major metropolitan areas, this is routine in cases of violent death, even with an obvious suicide. Because even when they are sure of the cause of death, they want to know what's going on in there. By examining the intestines, they can say what he had at his last meal. If he took an overdose, they can say how long ago.

I've been present for a few autopsies, which can be anything from a visual examination to an examination of the body fluids, to a complete autopsy. In the case of suicide, most are complete. This means that the suicide will be transported by the medical examiner (or coroner) to the county or city morgue. If it's after hours, sometimes he'll spend the night or the whole weekend—naked on a stainless steel cart in a refrigerated room.

After the brain and vital organs are removed from the body, they are placed in a plastic bag and put back into the body cavity. Then the body is rough-stitched back up and sent to the funeral home. (Of course, everybody knows intellectually that the guy is dead. And while I know these things intellectually myself, having seen them, it is still not how I would wish to wind up.)

Outside, a late-model car comes roaring up and screeches into the deceased's driveway, which can only mean that the car contains a relative or friend. I had already talked to this woman on the car phone, on the way out to the scene, trying to discourage her from coming to the house for at least another hour or so.

She jumps out of her car, still hurrying.

"Is he...?"

"Yes, ma'am. He is dead."

"Did he...?"

"Well, while I can't say for sure, there is every indication that, yes ma'am, he hung himself."

"Can I...?"

"No, ma'am, you can't go in there. Not until the crime scene people are through, the medical examiner has come and gone, and his wife has come to take possession of the house. You don't want to go in there anyway. There's nothing in there you can do."

She breaks down for a moment. I hold onto her shoulders until she gets a grip.

She recovers her composure, gets on her car phone.

And the ripples start to spread.

Even when it's not a close friend or relative, no matter how gently delivered, being notified of a suicide is like a kick in the stomach. Even if they thought they saw it coming, they're never ready.

The secretary in his office, whom it has fallen to me to both notify and get further information from, is no exception.

Tears streak her face. Her mother has come down to the office to be with her. And it turns out that I already know both of them. I tell her—confirm for her, which is even more important—that Frank J. is dead, and that it was probably self-inflicted. You'd be surprised how important that firm confirmation really is. It gives them some relief, usually, because it gives them at least one thing they can be certain of.

"Do you know when he did it?"

"Probably late yesterday or last night."

"Did he do it in the house? He had a hole in the ceiling where he'd fallen through from the attic one time, and there were some rafters there—is that how?"

"Yes, ma'am."

"I'm glad I didn't see it when I went out. I stuck my head in the window, but I didn't see anything."

Between bouts of crying, she begins to pour out the story of the last days of Frank J.

After a while the office phone rings. Her mother answers it, then hands it to me. It's Frank's soon to be ex-wife. I take that back: it's Frank's widow. I had spoken to her earlier, before going to the scene, and must now confirm her suspicions.

"Yes ma'am, the best information we have is that it was self-inflicted, by hanging."

"Is there any chance it was anything else?"

"No, I don't believe so. Please understand that the medical examiner is the one who makes the final ruling, but from what I saw, I would not be comfortable saying that it was anything other than intentional. He left a note."

"What did it say?"

"I didn't read the note, but you'll be able to see a copy of it."

"What about the house?"

"Have you filed for divorce?"

"Yes."

"Is it final?"

"No."

"When our people walk out, they'll secure it. Once they have concluded interviews with neighbors, and they are satisfied that it was self-inflicted, we'll be finished with the house and all the properties. When I left, they had just called for the mortuary service to take him to the Medical Examiners's office. Let me give you a little more information. The first thing you need to do is decide which funeral home you are going to use. If you need any help with any of this, feel free to call me. Anything we can help you with, let me know. I also suggest you talk to your lawyer."

The details, both big and small, are just beginning for Mrs. Frank J.

Now, here comes the guilt. It's unjustified, perhaps, but it hurts just the same.

And back in the office, the phone rings again.

This time, it's about an earlier suicide, Larry S., also thirty-eight. He was an old friend. I'd known him almost all his life, and much of my own. He had attended my church. I'd baptized him, and about twenty years ago, I had married him. This is his wife on the phone. With all her other problems, she's got to worry about the upcoming memorial service too. She wants me to officiate.

Since I knew him personally, even more than usual I wonder about his last moments—what was going on in his mind, before he pulled the trigger. Was he picturing himself at the funeral? Or was he thinking, they'll be happier with me out of the picture?

What *was* that last thought—the one he blew so completely and irretrievably away? Sad to say, the only thing we can know about his last thought is that it was greatly influenced by alcohol.

Larry, in spite of being a good man and a hard worker most of his life, had developed a pretty solid drinking problem—to the point that you could no longer tell whether or not he had been drinking at all. More and more toward the end, drinking became his biggest problem.

At the end, it was a huge one.

There had been a fight. A big one—but it shouldn't have been a fatal one. To cool off, his wife had left the house for several hours. When she came back, he was gone. She thought maybe he'd finally listened and checked into rehab. But he wasn't there, either.

After a day or so more, she became really worried about him. She called the police. She called friends where he might be staying. She called her family.

A week passed.

Then, one afternoon, her father came over to check on her, to see if she'd heard anything.

And there, in the yard, he found him.

He had been there all along. After the fight, apparently *right* after the fight, he had crawled over a fence and into a little wooded area behind the house, laid down in some weeds, and shot himself with a .38.

I've told his widow she didn't kill him, and that leaving that day was exactly the right thing to do.

Even if you set aside my own feelings about alcohol, the fact remains that the suicide rate among alcoholics is a great deal higher than among that of the non-alcoholic population. Different studies result in different numbers. A study based on coroner's reports in two Eastern cities showed a ten-percent incidence of alcoholism in suicides. Other, more thorough investigations, in which close relatives of the suicides were interviewed, showed a thirty-percent incidence.

European studies have shown that as many as twenty-one percent of all alcoholics die from suicide.

Some studies put it even higher.

Regardless of the exact statistics, it is clear that there is a strong relationship between alcohol and suicide. As to why this is so, different interpretations yield different results.

Researcher William Rushing found data to support the idea that the alcohol-suicide connection lies in what I call a dwindling spiral: Excessive drinking causes alcoholics to neglect familial, occupational, or social roles, so that the alcoholic becomes more and more a social outcast—and the result of that pain and humiliation is that he drinks even more.

I have seen evidence to support that.

Experimental intoxication studies have also indicated that intoxication ALONE may be a crucial factor in suicide.

I have seen evidence to support that.

Karl Menninger forwarded the idea that alcoholism is a form of self-destruction used to avert—or to take the place of—the more drastic self-destruction of suicide.

I can support that.

Studies by George Murphy and Eli Robins in the late sixties through the late seventies showed that one-third of suicides suffering from alcoholism had experienced the loss of a close relationship within six weeks of their death.

I have seen that.

If there is a difference between alcoholic suicides and non-alcoholic ones, it may have been found by Ernest Palola. Palola found that alcoholic suicides were more frequently due to separation or divorce resulting from the problems of alcoholism, while non-alcoholic suicides were due more to the death of a loved one.

I have seen that, too.

And I think all of the above parties—Menninger, Robins, Murphy, Palola, et al—would agree with me on the cure for potential suicides, alcoholic and non-alcoholic alike.

It's a difficult cure, but it's also very simple.

Don't reach for a drink. Don't reach for a gun. Reach for the phone.

That rings true.

Simplistic, sloganistic perhaps, for someone who is suicidal. There is all that self-loathing, that hopelessness. The self-loathing makes the phone weigh a ton, while the drink is feather light. And the drink makes the gun lighter, and lighter, and lighter... and pretty soon, it's so light and air-ish that it has just floated up into the hand...

But I know some people who can make that gun weigh

a million pounds. I know some folks that, if they are heard, could make that *phone* float to the ear. They are people who would give anything in the world to bring their loved ones back. They'd give almost as much to keep one living person, even a total stranger, from going.

In the strongest possible sense of the word, they're survivors.

They've survived the suicide of a loved one, and that's tough enough. They've also survived all the nightmares that accompany it, and that is even tougher.

Chapter 8

The taxpayers (you and I) pay them to deal with the parts of reality most of us do not wish to see: The gritty, hard, mean, savage streets, and the carnage which occurs on them. We deputize them to deal with the world that is deranged, dysfunctional, distorted and desperate; the world of the drunks and the junkies, the homeless and the heroin addicts, the crack killers and the crack killed. We turn over to them all responsibility for dealing with the red raw remains of mankind at its suicidal, homicidal, or just plain accidental, worst.

Most of us, as Joe Doe or Josephine Q. Public, only see ourselves in their mirrored sunglasses as we reach out irritably to take the traffic ticket. We see them only in terms of what they are "doing" to us; a uniform causing an interruption which will be followed by a legal hassle, something for our lawyer to fix.

We have better places to go; seldom do we reflect on the fact that it is because of them that we do not have to go to the worst places—and because of them that the worst places aren't any worse than they are.

If only you could see what they've seen, those eyes behind the sunglasses. And they see these horrors routinely; scenes from *The Inferno*, fodder for night-sweats to last them a lifetime that still get only a passing mention, or no mention at all, in the local papers or the nightly news, because the red raw death stemming from accidents, suicides, and single-victim homicides is "their" business.

The day shift may find them getting blessed-out by a motorist they've stopped for speeding and, ten minutes later, sorting through the broken-doll remains of a traffic accident.

Impact? There was one not long ago. A Hispanic family was coming back to the area from Mexico in a pickup truck and a camper shell with eleven people crowded into it when the driver fell asleep and hit a guardrail. Since four of them were killed, it got full coverage on the evening news. Lots of people said they saw me on the tube, comforting the family.

But I wasn't comforting the family at all. I was comforting a girl from up in Crime Scene. Her husband is also one of our officers; I'd married them. They have a little baby. And what the camera didn't pick up is that we were standing over the body of a little baby—about the same age as hers—hidden by some weeds.

People call them "cops." But they are also mothers and fathers, sisters and brothers, daughters and sons. Part of my job is to help them remember that someone else knows that, and cares.

Night shifts are sometimes rougher. As they pull out of the station into that long, eight-hour tunnel made by the headlights, police officers have no idea where it will take them. That is why the taxpayers (you and me and them) pay people like me: To keep them from losing their minds.

I do not mean "losing their minds" in the stereotypical sense.

I do not mean to self-aggrandizingly suggest that, were it not for me and people like me, these men and women in blue would one day all just jump out of the squad cars and go running down the street yelling and tearing their clothes off. No. I mean losing that part of themselves which they, being human, value the most: Their humanity. The part without which they might as well go crazy.

I feel terribly privileged, when I think about the singular way the Lord has doled and spaced out my blessings, opening my eyes only when I was ready to see, shaping my perspective only as fast as I could handle it, and allowing me to see the world around me in new ways.

I had spent thirty years as a pastor, doing regular pastoral duties. Marriages. Funerals. And Sunday sermons. I do not wish to minimize the struggles of those who follow that path all their lives. There is as much struggle and strife there, in many respects, as in any other job. But if I'd gone into full-bore chaplaincy straight out of the seminary, I don't think I would ever have developed an appreciation for just how different from "normal life" the lives of law enforcement officers really are, because it would soon have become normal for me, too.

I didn't start early and "harden" early. And thus I clearly see what it is each officer fears most and fights hardest: That he will fail to walk that shaky tightrope between too hard and too soft.

Most police officers enter the profession because they want to help others, even and especially those in the direst of straits and the worst of circumstances. They want to be in a position to protect the Good Guys from the Bad Guys, and to help the Good Guys when they are down. And maybe, just occasionally, help a Bad One become a Good One.

Though some would deny it, there is in most officers (and especially in the best ones) something of a bleeding heart. But the problem out on those mean streets is that if you let your heart bleed too much, it can soon bleed to death.

I want to help them find the best in themselves, and not let the worst in the world squeeze that out. I want to help them to the point where, at the end of their shift, they can go home feeling human without feeling too sad, or horrified—or feeling emotionally numb or disinterested.

Officer Jim Greenwell and I have a lot of things in common. We both like the job and the people. We both like a good joke and a good laugh.

And neither of us will ever forget the woman in the bathroom.

She'd fallen into a very small space, between the sink and the wall, so that she was wedged into a lifelike sitting position. Instead of looking very dead, which she was, she looked more as if she had just somehow sat down in there and gotten stuck, and would get up at any moment. It was eerie.

But mostly, the eeriness was because of the face.

Through a trick of human physiognomy and blast dynamics, something rather unusual had happened: Her face looked surprised, perhaps, but intact, while the head that should have been supporting the face—the cheekbones, the cranium, the jaw, the bones of the palate— was blown away by the self-inflicted blast from a 30-06.

It was a face up to about the hairline, standing all by itself there on top of a chin.

Maybe that's why our gaze, no matter how hard we fought the impulse, kept drifting back to the face: It shouldn't have been there. It should have been blown off. And if it weren't, it should still have responded to gravity at some point by folding in on itself and becoming part of the horrendous yet anonymous damage.

I think if that had been the case, Jim Greenwell would not have given it much more than a second thought. As a crime scene officer, he has been to some of the absolute worst, with never a quiver.

But from time to time, he still comes into my office and talks about that one. And I listen.

Because, in a nutshell, that's my job: To help them get through it at the scene—and after that, to help them for as long as it haunts them.

And this one still haunts Jim Greenwell.

"To this day," Greenwell recalls, looking back at those mental images, "I can't say what it was about that one. What it was about that scene, about that woman. It was just spooky. Yeah, sure, maybe it was that face with nothing to hold it up—but I've worked things like that before; it wasn't anything I hadn't seen before. In fact, I'd worked several like that one; it wasn't even as graphic as some of them. This wasn't the worst as far as the extent of damage. When you take a high-power at close range to the head, usually there's not going to be much of anything left besides a neck.

"So I don't know if it was that, or a combination of things. It may also have been that the room was so small, there wasn't much of anywhere to look. It's better if you can just look away at something else from time to time, but there was just nowhere else to look. And I was in such close proximity. I had to straddle her to take the facial photos.

"But I knew, the minute I started taking the pictures. I just knew it was going to get to me. Remember? I even talked about it at the time. I even told you: 'Chaplain, I just feel as if she's gonna reach up and grab my leg.' I've talked about it I don't know how many times. I can't even look at the pictures. That scene still scares me."

I don't know how to feel about this, how to think about it, exactly. I try to imagine what that woman must have been going through, what could have been so bad that this was her only way out, how it could have been so bad that, as a last act, she'd put her face in a total stranger's nightmares.

My job in these circumstances is two-fold, to go back and forth to the crime scene officers and the family.

With the officers, my counseling on the scene may be as simple as mere distraction, just talking about other things, normal things, to serve as a touchstone with reality, reminding them that they have lives and associations beyond the present grisly circumstances. I watch the officers for signs of overexposure or fixation on grisly details, and when I judge they've had too much, I urge them to take a break, get some air outside, or come out and talk.

Given the nature of their duties, the officers get to leave the situation behind fairly soon. But for the family, the nightmare may go on for years.

And this was one of the worst. Usually, I can offer them some hope, or at least some guidance, about what comes next, what to expect, what they should do.

But the family in this case was two handicapped young girls, both afflicted with cerebral palsy. They were home when their mother shot herself. They saw her, saw that same face that today gives a big, strong policeman his worst nightmares.

One of them, the younger, probably aged twelve or

thirteen, was so afflicted she could not talk. The older one, of high school age, could talk but was nearly paraplegic. In fact, she had placed her feet against that bathroom door in the hysterical fear that the thing inside would somehow come out.

We had to carry both of the girls out of that apartment in our arms.

As long as I live, I will never forget what that little older girl said to me, after the hysteria had passed. She said, "Mister, somewhere in this world, I got a daddy, but I don't know where he is. And I got a stepdaddy who doesn't love me. I've got a dead mother in there. And I've got this little sister who can't even talk. What in the world am I going to do? What's going to become of me?"

Tears just flowed down my face, right there.

Many times I have felt angry or frustrated with the people who have killed themselves—I always am, a little bit, and I certainly was then.

We carried the two little girls to the police car. I am sure child welfare took over from there.

But I'll never know what happened to them; I suspect that it was probably not anything very wonderful.

And I also think I know exactly what kind of horror still inhabits their nightmares to this very day.

Sometimes the mind-boggling contradictions inherent in the job of notifying people that their loved ones are dead become a little overwhelming.

I am a messenger of death who wants nothing more than to help the survivors try to get on with their lives. I am their worst nightmare, knocking on their door, yet hoping there'll be some way I can help them sleep a little easier.

I bring them the greatest wound it's likely they'll ever receive, and presume to hope to help heal them.

Sometimes, after a really bad one, where I've had to just about cut the planet out from under a mother's feet, when I've had to finish the job some suicidal son or drunk driver started, I wonder how much more I can take.

Two things keep me going, at those times.

One is the thought that someone else, someone with less practice and concern, might do a worse job of the telling. And the belief that, as far as I can tell, there is only one thing worse than someone like me coming to tell people the terrible truth, and that is their finding it out themselves. Better they should find out from someone like me than stumble on it unawares.

On the worst days in this job, that can happen more than once.

Two young boys had been riding their motorcycle in an undeveloped city park. Neighbors had complained. The trails had been roped off but they didn't see the cable until it was too late.

One of the boys was dead on arrival. Doctors were fighting to save the other boy when the father of one of the boys arrived. He had not been notified, but when his usually punctual son had not come home, the father had become concerned and checked the hospitals.

He asked to see the boy the doctors were working on, and we took him in. He looked at the boy, covered with blood, bruises and bandages, and said, "That's my son." He asked the doctors if the boy was going to die; the doctors, working feverishly, told him that it was very serious, but that the boy had a chance. At that point we had to leave the area so that the doctors could work unimpeded.

Slightly relieved, the father said that, since he knew most of his son's friends, he might be able to identify the dead boy.

We took him into the room where a little boy who'd had a tracheotomy lay. The trache was still open.

And the man took a look and, in a terribly somber voice, said, "*That* is my son."

I said, "Sir, it can't be. You just identified the other boy."

"Well, I made a terrible mistake, then. *That* is my son."

And it was.

I went straight from that sad situation back to the station and checked in with the dispatcher, who had paged me.

"What have you got?" I asked.

I was saddened on several levels by the ensuing exchange.

The dispatcher said: "A suicide, Chaplain, probably one of your former church members."

And I said, "What's the name?"

And then she said, "Bryan McQuirk."

I hated to squelch her good-intentioned and healthy levity with cold-water truth, but I had to say, "Yes, he was."

Much more than that, I hated the news.

Chapter 9

Once in some unlucky lifetimes the world takes a sudden sidestep and reality does a 180-degree turn, and everything you depended upon is no longer there. Life's underpinnings, the million little assumptions we all live with and depend on, are all yanked violently away. Life, after a moment like this, is never, ever going to be the same, because Life As You Knew It is forever gone.

Brent McQuirk and his wife, Lou Wayne, faced such a moment. Lou Wayne faced it first, and in a sense was the luckier of the two.

They'd just been out to eat, and had returned to their large and comfortable north Arlington home. Lou Wayne remembers coming down the hall to her son Bryan's room. She saw the gun first, leaning up against the bed, and she wondered aloud what it was doing in his room.

And then she came through the door and past the chest of drawers that had obstructed her view, and saw Bryan. She was luckier than her husband only because the shock reached out and slapped her so hard that she spun dizzily around and out of the room—and thus looked no more. In fact, that would be the last time she would ever see him.

She began to scream. It was a horrible scream. Not the scream of a woman confronted with a minor unpleasantness or sudden surprise, but a scream torn from the very roots of the soul, the searing scream of a woman whose world has disappeared. It brought her husband running up the stairs, down the hall, to the door, and into that room.

Shock was harsher to him. It reached out clammy hands

and pinned him motionless by the door. It held his eyes wide open and through them the horror poured in the fullest possible measure—horror to last a lifetime.

The shock did something else to Brent that it had not done to his wife. It made a sort of mental videotape of the scene, one that Brent McQuirk has absolutely no control over. In fact, as the years have passed, that tape has played itself in slow motion and agonizing detail at precisely the times he needed them least—during moments of stress. During, for example, board meetings. It has caused him to fall apart in those moments. In fact, for several years Brent believed that he might end his days in a madhouse.

Bryan McQuirk was by almost all accounts a perfect son, all that a parent could ask for. And his was not a pretentious, self-conscious perfection; it was not manipulative.

"It wasn't like he was putting on a show, and it wasn't a matter of him being too good to be true," recalled Brent McQuirk—who, in his own quiet way, may be one of the bravest men I know. Over the years he has many times, at my request, exhumed his awful experiences for the benefit of other, more recent suicide survivors, both singly and in groups.

There are several sad ironies in his tale, the greatest being that Bryan was not the "type," if there is such a thing, to commit suicide, and his relationship with his parents was warm and whole and good. He could talk with them about his problems, and did.

He even talked freely about the problem that drove him to his own self-destruction, or at least precipitated it. And the problem itself only proves the contention that Bryan McQuirk was a nice kid.

He was popular at school—but he was also something more. Where some in his age range sought friendships so they could appear popular, Bryan had friends because he was generally truly concerned about people. And many of his friends were similar to him—outgoing, fun-loving.

Brent McQuirk says with the clarity of hindsight, that

if his son had come to him and asked him what to do about a close friend, in retrospect he would have told him to do other than he did. But then Bryan didn't come to him at the outset. He didn't feel he needed to. He had been taught to do what he thought was right, and so he did it. He went to his friend's mother and told her about his concerns.

And things went downhill from there.

From a global perspective, one can probably make the case that teen suicide results not only from the fact that it's rough to be a teenager, but also from the fact that teenagers are rough on teenagers. This is particularly true in those social pressure cookers we call public schools. Bryan could not have foreseen the result of his good intentions, which was to be judged as a tattletale.

The outgoing, popular Bryan had attempted to do his friend some good, and suffered for it.

Should this have led someone to suicide? Well, the obverse of that question is should anything? It is easy to denounce Bryan's travails as a tempest in a teapot, but sometimes it's awfully hard to see when you're in the teapot looking out.

He was, in other words, in a pretty typical teenage bind.

None of this was any secret to his parents.

"We were aware of the situation," recalls Brent McQuirk. "He'd told us about what was going on, and we'd talked about it. We told him we would support him in any way we could."

Brent remembers that, one day not too long before it happened, he'd passed his son's bedroom and seen him sitting on the edge of the bed, staring into space. "I could see that he was really troubled. I sat down next to him to talk, and he just started crying. I remember going through some Scripture with him.

"If there were other issues, we didn't find them. There were no other issues that anyone has brought forward. We tried to find out what else, if anything, might have been going on with Bryan, anything that would shed some light on his death. But no one would talk to us about it."

On the walls of the hall leading to Bryan's room are photos of a handsome, solid, muscular-looking young man, a young man with his "head screwed on straight." Here's the one where he had his hair permed for the lead in *Oklahoma*. Here he is at his summer job at Six Flags, where he worked on a ride called The Shock Wave. Here he is with his old Ford Mustang.

It was down this same hall that the paramedics carried him.

Outsiders find it remarkable—the calm with which Brent and Lou Wayne McQuirk face their dead son's room.

If there are ghosts here, they are not the chain-rattling, horrifying kind, but the gentle memories of a good son whose emotions went suddenly wildly wrong—and then a life was no more.

And as Brent McQuirk stands at the doorway, looking at the furniture, still pretty much as it was ten years ago, the mental videotape begins to play.

Brent says that television and motion picture dramatizations of post-traumatic stress syndrome—the slow-motion stuff, the weird dissolves—are almost exactly what he sees on that screen inside his head. "They've got it right," he says.

And that tape is in Technicolor, with the predominant color being red—red everywhere. On the floor, walls, ceiling, desk, bed.

Red, red, red, where everything was beige or brown before.

Bryan was face down on the desk. He had taken a sixteen-gauge shotgun, held it at an upwards angle to his right cheekbone, and pulled the trigger.

Months later, as they attempted to repair the damage to the room, they would still find shotgun pellets in the ceiling.

"I thought that it must have blown the front of his face off, because he was face down, and his head looked like a basketball that was half inflated; his face was completely flattened against the desk. We found out later, after we'd buried him, that it was more intact than we had thought and that we might have had an open-casket funeral..."

Bryan's parents' nightmares were only just beginning,

as with most survivors—and one is tempted to call them "victims" instead. For the next several hours and days events unfolded behind a gray, misty wall of unreality, of shock. As unpleasant as this state is, I believe it beats the alternative. It's a built-in shock absorber. I don't think a human being could stand all the pain of these circumstances if he were forced to face it all at once. Even with this emotional filter in place, he's hurting badly enough.

Some describe the feeling in the immediate wake of the suicide of a loved one as being very physical, like the shock of a gunshot wound, or being hit hard with a sledgehammer. Brent McQuirk says, "It just rips your guts out. Literally. The pain is physical. It feels like something came along and took a great big bite out of your stomach."

The big gray cloud settling over the heart and mind also swallows some of your memory. McQuirk recalls only in the vaguest sense events following his wife's discovery of their son—the call to police, my arrival, and other friends, relatives and church members who came trickling in to build an emotional circle around the couple as the word spread.

The numbness and shock dissipates very slowly, very gradually. It was several days after the funeral that Brent and Lou Wayne were self-possessed enough to begin tentatively asking themselves those questions common to all suicide survivors. Why? Why did he do it?

The Why is almost never an answerable one; it stays with most survivors for the rest of their lives as they try and reject various theories. In the case of Bryan, it was all the more difficult since he'd been such a model offspring.

It has been more than ten years since Bryan committed suicide, and still the parents torture themselves with questions like, "If we'd *made* him go out to eat with us, would it have happened?"

Says Brent McQuirk, "For us, it will always be one of those things where, 'If I'd done this; I should've done that; I shouldn't have done the other.' But how do you ever know? I mean, if you ask, 'Would you like to go out to eat with us?' and he says no, you don't ordinarily say, 'Why? Hey—are you thinking about killing yourself?'"

The little half-clues and innuendoes left after most suicides are almost satanically tantalizing to the survivors. For instance, when they found Bryan, the phone was off the hook. Who had he been talking to? About what? His parents will never know.

Then there was the note, itself ambiguous: "I can't take it any more." What *it*? Even if Bryan had left a ten-page, single-spaced typewritten note detailing the sources of all the pressures he felt, it still wouldn't help his parents and other survivors to understand how these pressures were sufficient to produce in a normal young man the determination necessary to end his life. No problem, for his parents, could have justified his resolution of it.

If each man's individual extinction is inconceivable to himself, the same pretty much applies to loved ones, particularly one with no prior history of mental or emotional difficulty—and the natural human tendency is therefore to conclude that he really didn't mean to kill himself, and to search for evidence to support that conclusion.

The first hope was the autopsy—routinely, unceremoniously and impersonally performed on the body by county-paid pathologists. What the McQuirks hoped was that the scalpel would uncover some abnormality, a tumor or undetected lesion in the brain that had led to this bizarre hope. And it was in this hope that Brent McQuirk steeled himself to wade through the grim surgical details of the further indignities imposed on the ravaged body of his son.

But there were no abnormalities—at least, nothing that could be detected in the tissues which remained.

Finally, as a means of mentally saving face, Brent McQuirk seized on the shotgun his son had used. It belonged to Brent.

"I would think about that shotgun, and remind myself that it had a real light 'hair-trigger.' And I would say, 'He was just playing, just *fantasizing* about suicide, and he was holding that gun up to his head and saying, 'What if...' and he just barely touched that trigger and then..."

Maybe. Maybe not—and it is that unanswerable ambiguity that forever makes the question a form of torture.

"Because then," Brent McQuirk sighs, "what I have to remind myself next is that, whatever the reason, he's still gone."

The Why will always be out there, circling in the darkness, forever unanswered.

The second question the McQuirks and others ask is, "How will I get through this?" This does have an answer, albeit not an easy one. The answer is, day by day. You may not feel better tomorrow than you do today. But maybe by this time next year...

Brent McQuirk's problem is not atypical. He asks, "How do you face the mental tape that keeps playing? I don't guess you do. I had a lot of very serious psychological problems with that for a long time. I guess it finally came down to a form of what is called Post Traumatic Stress Syndrome. Probably not to the extent that soldiers had it in Vietnam—but on the other hand, the bodies those men saw over there weren't those of their sons, were they?

"And so the tape would just start. When I was under stress it would click in, and I'd just trip out, no matter where I was, and often in situations where I couldn't afford to trip out—in the middle of a board meeting, at the most inopportune times. It became apparent to those around me that I needed professional help.

"There was a suggestion that I needed to go into a hospital, but I couldn't handle that. I chose to do outpatient therapy. It wasn't easy. First of all, there's the matter of getting past the guilt, and all the 'whys.' It marks you. As a parent, if your child kills himself, you're a failure, wearing a big neon sign that says, "Loser Father." I felt even more foolish in our immediate circle of friends because of all the times I had bragged on Bryan—about what a good kid he was, about how he never got into any trouble.

"Somehow, because you're a parent, it becomes all your fault: I should have done this, not done that, and 'What did I do way back when to set up the psychological mindset that might have contributed to it?'"

And, because the family has a strong traditional Christian commitment, there was another question waiting to tear at Brent McQuirk's turbulent heart: Did Bryan go to hell?

"I had to deal with that: Is suicide an unpardonable sin? Some believe it is. Our reliance had been on the saving grace of Jesus Christ, that he forgives you for everything, past, present and future, and that the only unpardonable sin is refusing to accept that grace.

"I remember one day on my way to work I happened to be listening to a preacher on the radio. This preacher came on and started talking about suicide, and how cowardly it was, and how God would never forgive it. I will never forget that. It just wiped me out. I fell apart. After a long time, finally, at least in my own mind, I settled the issue. Bryan had made a mistake, a permanent one, but one that God could forgive."

Why was this question so important to Brent McQuirk?

Part of his initial therapy had occurred under the supervision of a therapist who encouraged him to pretend that Bryan was present in the room, and to tell Bryan his feelings; tell Bryan everything he wanted to.

"I did it mostly privately, in my quiet time, sometimes vocally and out loud, sometimes in my head. At first, it was, 'Why were you so *stupid*! Didn't you know that all you had to do was come to us, come to *me???*'"

And for a long time, that was the tenor of it.

But then one day, Brent found himself sitting in his son's room. He goes there, sometimes, to talk to Bryan. He found himself saying: "I understand. I'm very sorry you did it. And I'm very much looking forward to telling you that, and to talking about it all someday."

He longs to tell Bryan that IN PERSON. On the other side after, hopefully, a long lifetime. Because that's how long this kind of pain lasts—a lifetime.

Chapter 10

Just as there are numerous myths surrounding suicide, so there are around suicide survivorship. This is particularly difficult when the one who kills himself is someone who is abusive to friends and family; someone everyone wishes would just "go away."

The general perception in such a case is that the immediate family is "better off without him." Empirically and externally, that may be so. There will be no more abuse. There will be no more misery emanating from his actions. There will never be heard another discouraging word.

But better off? It depends on your perspective.

Take the case of Virginia R., a Dallas executive secretary, a bright, sunny, sensible woman who generally has a smile for everyone and is comfortable with almost every subject—except that of her father, who killed himself.

A big, domineering, manipulative man, Virginia's father craved approval from, control over, and submissiveness of his family. Approval he got in public, mainly in church; control and submissiveness he got at home, via religion.

At home, he was both physically and verbally abusive, sparing neither the rod nor the tongue-lashing to convince his wife and children of their inferiority and their wickedness. What he wanted was always wise and just; what the other family members wanted was invariably sinful and the work of the devil.

Some circumstantial evidence indicates that he sexually abused at least one of his daughters, one of the younger ones. The other family members suspected it, and as the girl grew older, she became promiscuous and began to show other signs of low self-esteem.

The man insidiously used religion as one of his means of control. He was "big" in his church, which was part of one of the fringe fundamentalist groups. Not out of the strength of his faith, but out of his desire for control, he insisted that his family adhere rigorously to its many prohibitions and requirements. Variance from the slightest of these was grounds for cruel punishment.

The very faith that should have provided them with an outlet for their misery became his means of achieving control. Further complicating matters was the fact that, in this sect, divorce was not merely frowned upon, but considered as anathema.

By the time her mother finally had taken enough and moved herself and her children out of the house—and by this time, the kids were almost grown—Virginia hated her father with a passion. Part of the hatred was for the things he'd done to her, for the abuse, and part of it was for what it left her with: a cowed feeling she has been struggling to overcome for most of her adult life. Steps that come easy for some—getting a job, dating, socializing—have been very hard for her because she'd come to believe that almost everything she could conceivably do was rooted in evil, and that if she enjoyed something, it must therefore be wrong.

Her parents' divorce was, all things considered, remarkably amicable. The husband, a deacon who was loved by all who didn't know him, seemed to take as much pleasure in appearing nobly wronged and unfairly aggrieved as earlier he had enjoyed bedeviling his family.

Virginia's mother remarried, and so, later on, did her father. Years passed without her ever seeing him.

Then one night, her mother called to tell her that he'd put a shotgun to his head.

While her mother talked and cried over the phone, Virginia waited for the shock to hit. There was none.

And then she waited for the grief. It didn't come.

And then she found herself hoping for at least a kind of wistfulness, a vague pity for a mean, cruel, and duplicitous man who perhaps could not help himself because of childhood trauma of his own.

She could get to that point—but only intellectually, not emotionally. Emotionally, she felt only a vast indifference and a kind of mild gloating that the scorpion had finally turned and stung itself to death.

She did not attend the memorial service.

"I didn't cry over him then," she says, "and I haven't cried over him yet."

But she is not proud of this. While she never cries over him, she sometimes cries over the fact that she can't.

She shouldn't, of course. She probably should just be thankful that, in spite of his example and his abuse, the mean manipulativeness wasn't transferred from him to her.

The best test of her humanity lies in the fact that, after relief, there came guilt over the relief. And that is the tough part for survivors in cases such as these: The guilt. Grief, though a powerful force, is something that can be expiated, over time.

But guilt hounds some survivors for the rest of their lives.

And then there is the myth about "turning lemons to lemonade," where it is perceived that, sad though the suicide may have been, it served as a catalyst to drive the survivor to heights he might otherwise not have attained.

"Too bad about old So-and-So's kid," they'll tut, "but if it hadn't happened, he wouldn't be where he is today."

This misperception, while well-meaning, is doubly cruel to the survivor. First, it incorrectly attributes the survivor' success to the absolute worst thing that ever happened to him, crediting the tragedy—rather than the survivor's strength at overcoming it—for any good that may have occurred.

More horrifying to the survivor is that people believe he's enjoying his success and is thankful for the tragedy, when the truth is that life has lost its flavor and success is by no means sweet because he's lost the one person he would have wanted to share it with.

Every community has a case like this.

In Arlington, it's Kent Grusendorf.

Externally and superficially, Kent's life did change "for

the better" after his son's suicide nearly fifteen years ago—
but only depending upon how you keep score.

Observers on the outside looking in couldn't help but
notice that within a year of his son's death in 1979, the
previously apolitical and somewhat noncommittal
Grusendorf had become a powerful player in both politics
and the civic-service arena. By 1980 he was campaigning
for Reagan and embarking on a career of public service
that would find him on the board of dozens of community
organizations.

And in 1984 he successfully ran for the state legislature.

Theory 1: He simply put his son's death behind him
and got on with his life; he would have achieved these
things regardless.

Theory 2: His activism was a sort of living memorial.

Theory 3: His son's death made him aware that life is
short.

The truth is that Kent Grusendorf had to have
something to do. *Had* to. Didn't really matter what. With
his son dead, Grusendorf had lost his reason for living, for
doing. If he was going to live, he had to find another one.

To an external observer, if Grusendorf's life had been
"about" anything before the suicide, it had been about
money. In fact, if back then you'd asked *him* what he was
about, money would have been his answer. Grusendorf is
one of those quiet people who keeps his cards close to his
chest and his eye on the ball. He doesn't volunteer much,
but he listens very, very well. In any conversation, but
particularly in those concerning business, you get the
sense that if he doesn't have the advantage when the
conversation begins, he will by the time it's over—or
you'll think he does, which is pretty much the same thing.

By 1979, he was flying high, having parlayed his no-
nonsense personality and computer-like facility with
numbers into a thriving company—Syco Corp., a
manufacturer of precision aerospace components—and a
sizable fortune.

He also had a wife and a seventeen-year-old son. Life
was good.

And then the boy fell in love with a fifteen-year-old girl. Maybe, Grusendorf says, lovesick is a better word. The girl, who didn't return his affections to the same degree, left for Atlanta, Georgia, to visit relatives, and was only going to be gone for a couple of weeks. But the boy couldn't stand it.

He got in his car and ran away.

Grusendorf was later able to track the boy's movements by the gasoline credit-card charges he had run up. He'd made it to Atlanta, where he stayed a couple of days. Then he turned around and headed home—but got only as far as Cleveland before heading back to Atlanta again.

And then he headed home again.

Many, many survivors invent scenarios to DENY the fact that the death was a suicide and will even go to great lengths to "prove" that it was an accident or homicide, and not the "unthinkable." Some even go to the trouble of withholding evidence and interfering with police investigations to help themselves maintain this illusion.

Kent Grusendorf has a theory that his son's death was something other than suicide; that it was an effort to fake a suicide attempt—and there are some factors which give his theory credence.

First is the fact that, if it's true, it only worsens Grusendorf's guilt, offering him no easy outs. Grusendorf, who acknowledges that as a father he was a strict disciplinarian, believes his son felt he was in a great deal of trouble as a result of the nine-day trip, and may have thought that the only way to get back into the family home more or less scot-free was to throw a scare into his parents that would outweigh the anger.

Grusendorf believes his son chose an area of new construction only a few miles from home, figuring he could stand outside the car and leave the motor running—filling the car with carbon monoxide through a garden hose—so that when workers came into view early that morning he could just jump into his car and look like a young man who was trying to kill himself. Then they'd pull him out, revive him, and he would be restored to the bosom of the family, perhaps even indulged and given a longer leash.

Everything seems to have gone according to plan. Tracks indicate he'd walked around the car for quite some time; long enough, in fact, for it to overheat. He hopped in only when he saw the construction workers beginning to arrive.

The problem was that, rather than "rescue" him, the alarmed construction workers opted instead to call the police.

It takes only about five minutes under such circumstances for the carbon monoxide to produce unconsciousness. The car's motor had been running long enough to overheat, yet he was still alive by the time police got there, and he responded slightly when they tapped on the window. They pulled him out.

But carbon monoxide continues to bond with oxygen once it's in the bloodstream and by the time they got him to the hospital, he'd lapsed into a coma from which he did not recover. Four days later, he died.

After a suicide, particularly a youthful one, the bottom always seems to fall out of the close survivors' lives—but it was perhaps even worse in Grusendorf's case, since he soon realized what he had not consciously known while his son was alive—that the boy was his reason for living.

"I guess people probably do things more because of subconscious motives than reasons that they are actually aware of," Grusendorf recalls. "I had subconsciously been so involved with money so I could leave the money and the company to my kid. All of a sudden, I didn't have anybody to leave it to, and no reason for doing the things I had been doing. Prior to his death, all I had cared about was making money. After it happened, I didn't care about money—so I didn't really care about anything."

What Grusendorf is describing is not mere indifference, but a far worse lack of emotion—a death of emotion and interest that is utter apathy. For people in that condition, getting as high on the emotional chart as abject grief may actually be the best part of their day.

"I was bawling every day," Grusendorf says. "I was crying when I woke up in the morning and when I went to sleep at night."

On top of the grief, there was the unjustified guilt and the unreasonable blame to complicate matters.

"I would blame myself; you can't help but put some blame on yourself. I would second-guess various statements I'd made to him, little things, like, when he wanted to borrow my new Cadillac to go to the prom and I'd told him no.

"After he was gone, I'd tell myself, 'If I'd told him yes, he'd have had something to look forward to, and might have lasted to the prom.' Just little things like that that you second-guess yourself on. If, the time he'd asked this, if I'd answered it that way, would it have made a difference? ... and it's endless, because the answer's gone.

"I blamed my wife at the time and even the guy down the street. I'd see him walking down the street with his kids and I'd get mad at him. Why did he deserve to have kids, especially the mean little kids you meet around the neighborhood? Why, when I had such a perfect kid, does that one deserve to live?

"In other words, you find yourself becoming quite mean-spirited, in addition to the pain, and it gets to be quite a mess. You go through a lot of strange emotions."

His marriage was beginning to fall apart—"all the joy was gone from it"—and his business was carrying itself. "The momentum was carrying both me and it; the momentum carried me for maybe ten years after it happened. I was desperate for a distraction, something to take my mind off the loss and the pain.

"Business didn't seem important to me at all—for a long time, nothing's important. It was that way for about a year. I never had any intention of getting involved in politics, but I wasn't really working. I wasn't really doing anything, I wasn't taking care of business; I just kind of got involved to occupy my mind. In September of 1980, I got really involved in the Reagan campaign, as a diversion."

His work—aimed at helping youths—is close to Kent's heart. Though he's tried hard not to make the issue of suicide into a personal, save-the-world campaign, he has, at my urging, told the story of his personal tragedy to a few groups, and both donated to and spoken on behalf of my video, *Suicide is Not Painless*.

More meaningful to him than pure suicide prevention alone is the creation of an environment in which young people have cause to be hopeful about the future, rather than fatalistic.

Grusendorf, like me, took a dim view of some educational policies in the late seventies and early eighties, particularly those that preached inevitable nuclear annihilation. They were flat scaring kids to death back then. Grusendorf's son had at one point confided to his mother that he just wished they'd hurry up and get it over with, since the waiting was the worst part.

"I think that's a problem for a lot of kids: They don't see a future. The kids who tend to contemplate suicide are the ones who have a hopeless or helpless feeling, and global politics are certainly beyond their control.

"There was actually a 'nuclear curriculum' that was being promoted during that period, and I think some kids were the victim of that curriculum. So I sort of got involved in educational issues to some extent because of that—though I think time did more about that curriculum than I did."

Grusendorf served two years on the State Board of Education before his position changed from an elective to an appointed position.

All the laurels, the headlines, the name recognition. All the personal progress and growth that comes when a quiet and private man pushes himself into public life and politics; all this must be weighed against something else.

In Grusendorf's case, it is probably this:

"Within the past week alone, I woke up dreaming that I was holding my son in my lap, seeing him just as clear as can be. And then I realized he was still gone, and the feeling of unreality returned."

UNreality, he said. What was very real for him is gone. All that has come afterward is somehow thin, insubstantial, and hollow beside the reality of his son's death.

I asked Kent Grusendorf how he'd like to feel five years from now.

"I'm not sure what your question is," he said.

"How would you like to feel, relative to your son's suicide?"

"I'm not sure how to answer your question."

"Do you want the dreams to go away?"

"No, NO! I don't want the memory to go away. I wish we could turn back the clock fifteen years and have it all undone, but there isn't any second alternative. So I live with what I've got."

Better off?

Chapter 11

Instinctively, mothers are mostly about survival of their children—survival at all costs, under any circumstances, and no matter what the sacrifice.

Craig Christiansen didn't believe in a life after death—yet now he has one, after a fashion.

And I have to wonder: If he knew about this, would he like it? Is this the way he would have wanted it to be? Is this what he would have wanted for Mom?

Could this possibly be what he was after?

I first met Craig in a letter from his mother, Linda:

January 18, 1985
Dear Reverend Elliott,

His name was Craig. For almost nineteen years he lived and laughed and loved. Then he died—by his own hand, but he lives on in every life he ever touched. No sun will rise and set without the impact of knowing him being felt by those who live that day without him.

The memory floods my mind and seeps into the cracks of my broken heart every conscious moment of my life. I am his mother. His life came from me, and the end of that life is no less a part of me.

The year is 1985; January 18th is the first anniversary of his death; March 31st would have been the twentieth anniversary of his birth, and all the days & weeks & years in between we shared together—then he was gone. He lived among us for eighteen years, nine months, and eighteen days, so short a time to have known someone who had so much more time to live.

His memory must not die with that physical part of

his presence. He must live on, not to lend comfort to those of us who suffer our loss, but to send a message to those who may follow along his path.

And so I dedicate this message in your memory, Craig. *The most significant thing you did was to live, not to die. The memory you left behind was who you were while you were alive. You had a special quality, a warmth and beauty about you that was unique. Your life was precious and can never be replaced. No memory of you will substitute for your touch. One act of defiance, of rage, of pain, of weakness, robbed all of us of that precious life.*

And so I do not glorify your passing. I do not love or honor you more in death than I did in life. I ache for you, and yet, not just for my loss and pain, but for all the special moments you will never experience in this wonderful life. Your time on earth was too short for you to grow to know the wisdom or the value of one, single, glorious day, with all its promises of renewed hope.

Life—the most precious gift of all, your father & I gave you. I heard your first cry, my son, but not your last. My prayer is that somewhere, somehow, there is a life which may pass through that moment of agony, and choose to live on. It is my living legacy to you, Craig.

Good-bye, son; in my heart I feel your smile, and I am at peace with the feeling that you know how much I love you.

Mom

I finally met Linda one dreary, drizzly day in December, but in the bland commercial cheerfulness of Denny's, Linda Christiansen and I are getting all fired up on caffeine and conversation.

I had liked Linda Christiansen from her letter alone, and like her even more in person. She's a bright, energetic, and articulate attorney specializing in criminal law. She's more youthful than her forty-eight years (and far more than my fifty-seven), and has started her second family; she has a five-year-old son.

Every survivor of suicide shows both positive signs and negatives. Linda Christiansen is, like most others, quite a mix. Positive, negative. Encouraging, discouraging. Cause for hope. Maybe cause for concern.

Because at least once, I wondered who it was that I was really talking to.

That may have been my fault. I asked to speak to Craig.

The policeman had come to her door nearly nine years earlier, on January 18, 1984. He was a young officer, not too much older than Craig, who was then nineteen. The minute she opened the door, she knew it was about her son. The minute the officer sat her down on the couch and took her hand, she knew that Craig was dead. With the eerie calm that shock produces, she whispered, "Car wreck?"

"No ma'am," said the officer, shaking with a case of nerves that bearers of death messages can appreciate, "it appears that he shot himself."

Some of the facts in Craig Christiansen's case seem to square with what researchers have come to believe about youthful suicide, based on statistical studies.

First, he was from a broken home. While broken homes are no more common among suicidal adolescents than their non-suicidal peers, the divorced parents of suicidal adolescents are much more likely to remarry, and remarry soon. There is also frequently a history of changes of residence and other disruptive events somewhere in the background. And alcohol abuse as a means of dealing with the problems is frequently a factor.

Craig had a history that included all of these. (And please remember that having all of these and then some is still no guarantor of individual suicide—only a reflection of statistical trends). As the field of suicidology progresses, the experts may further narrow the statistical focus and learn about the personality types of the parents of suicides.

Linda Christiansen and her former husband had married in 1965. Craig was born a few months later. Linda was nineteen, and concedes that, given the disparate personalities, the marriage was never a perfect match.

Where she was voluble and gregarious, he was reserved,

tending to withhold his feelings. "He wasn't cold and unfeeling; he was just not in touch with himself. He was and is a good man. He was a good provider—there was nothing he wouldn't go to the moon to get for you—but he was never able to give very much emotionally."

But while acknowledging the frustrations of their personality differences, she puts all of the blame for the split on her own shoulders. Because of the nature of his job, the family moved around a lot. And everywhere they went, Linda continued her education.

"I guess," she says, "I wanted more than I already had, which was a lovely family. So I kept on going to school. And when I finally was through, and already in my early thirties, he encouraged me to go on to law school. I remember asking him, 'How old am I gonna be when I get out of law school?' He asked, 'Well, how old are you gonna be if you don't go?' He was very supportive, so I went on."

It was a heady and challenging environment, and it absorbed Linda Christiansen completely. In early mid-life, a whole new world was opening up before her—a world in which she felt she could make both her mark and a difference. Soon her marriage paled in comparison to the broader life she felt beckoning.

"By the time I got out of law school, I'd lost touch with him. It just wasn't there. And I wanted to get on with my career and, well, my own self-importance. It just happened. I got out of law school, graduated in late 1981, became licensed in May 1982; he and I separated and by the end of September 1982, the divorce was final."

Linda Christiansen maintains that her ex-husband was deeply hurt in the process.

"I think he believed and hoped that with time I'd get through this phase and come back, and the family would be back together. Then he realized, after we filed, after the division of property, that we would not get back together."

Hindsight tells her that her son held on to that hope of reconciliation, also.

However, once reality set in, the ex-husband quickly

set about finding someone to fill the emotional void. "He found someone, and the kids liked her a lot. But in the middle of this relationship he started seeing someone else, and the kids didn't like her as well." This woman was married but separated; as soon as the divorce was final, shortly after New Years Day, 1984, they got married. Craig did not particularly like her, which was unfortunate."

When the Christiansens had split, Linda had moved to a condo only five minutes away from the family home. Since it was home base for both Craig and his younger sister Lori, both remained there with their father.

Craig was, in fact, living there when his father took his new wife on a honeymoon.

Linda Christiansen says she should have seen it coming. On account of the drinking.

"For one reason or another, I wasn't aware of how severe it was. I knew Craig drank, and I knew the drinking had started about the time of the divorce—but that was also the age at which young men traditionally start to drink with increased social acceptance. I don't feel like he drank very frequently—but when he would drink, he would almost always drink to the point of passing out. This had happened two or three times. That I knew. And one of the hardest parts of going through the guilt process was my refusal to recognize the seriousness of the problem.

"I do believe that if there had been intervention early on, to cover that problem, the others might not have come up. There is a strong possibility that this would not have happened. But all I did about it was talk to him, taking the motherly role of, 'Don't do this,' but I didn't seek outside help, I didn't intervene in the classic sense. I should have, because it was a sign."

And so it appears that Craig Christiansen just flat got drunk and killed himself.

On the day of his death, a Wednesday, he had been to school at Tarrant County Junior College, and got out early in the afternoon. He and his buddies went to the house and hauled out a fifth of scotch. By the time the friends left, Craig Christiansen was screaming, bug-eyed, wall-banging, out-of-his-mind drunk.

And that fact will always be both a burden and a consolation to Linda Christiansen.

It is a burden because she believes she should have intervened.

It is a consolation because she believes her son was so drunk that he didn't know what he was doing at the time—in essence, that he didn't mean to kill himself, at least in the volitional, pre-meditated sense of the word. And that allows her to cling to the hope that maybe her son's life had not become relentlessly, chronically awful because of the domestic situation.

Very often, survivors do find some straw of hope to cling to—but this is a larger straw than most; she has some hard data to back her up.

"Whether right or wrong, I believe in my heart he didn't intend to end his life. I saw the autopsy report; his blood alcohol was .29 at the time it was measured, and it had dissipated somewhat from what it was at the time of the suicide. Since I practice law and do a lot of DWI work, I've learned a lot about blood alcohol levels. In a person of his age, tolerance, health, weight, and heart-rate, he would have been comatose, and alcohol poisoning would have occurred at about .29. I think it would be ludicrous to assume that he had much control over his faculties at that point.

"To say that he was out of his mind is not just an excuse to placate my own feelings, but is a scientific fact.

"He certainly had enough presence of mind to navigate down the hall to his father's bedroom to get the gun, which was already loaded, and go back to his room and do what he did. But I don't believe he had the presence of mind to plan this out, figure out how he was going to do it, or understand the consequences of what he would do to us. He hadn't made those kinds of decisions. But it happened. He' s still gone."

Yet in one rather disquieting way, he's not.

Perhaps not by a long shot.

The line between remembrance and obsession is not only fine, it's also indistinct. And in this case, it is either a line that Linda Christiansen enjoys trying to walk—or is compelled to.

Her first reaction, after the officer left her home that day, was the usual: "Shock, not unlike that of a gunshot wound, where it's happened but you don't really believe it's happened. Then the first thought that I was aware of, almost immediately, was Lori, my daughter, who was fifteen at the time. I guess, as far as my own survival, it was tied up in how do I help her, what do I do to put her life back together?

"That was the immediate need—and that, more than anything else, is the one thing that over nine years has not changed—my desire to protect her. That somehow, whatever I have to give must be brought to bear on that problem. Lori, that's the life that went on, and that was my survival point. It never occurred to me that I would not survive, because I had that life dependent on me. It gave me a purpose, a going-on reason.

"Other than that, though, there was a complete shutdown. Even though I could walk you through events, even conversations, when it comes to thoughts and feelings, I can't, because there's that shutdown, that block. I guess that's just the body's natural process; the memory is distorted.

"I can tell you I felt shock and disbelief and pain. I can use the words, but I can't make you feel them. I really can't."

Lori, younger, more resilient and, after all, a sister rather than a mother, progressed faster.

"It hit her hard, but she was very emotional—able to cry and talk and express outwardly. She was in that state of shock, time-wise, much less than I. Very soon she was accepting that he was gone. And she was the first to be able to say, 'We knew he had a drinking problem, we knew he was upset, we should have seen this coming.' She was the first to begin to absorb the loss and the guilt, and then the blame—to talk about what we should have done."

Craig's father may have taken it the hardest. He took all the pictures down, sent all mementos of Craig to Linda, and to this day, does not talk about his son.

For Linda Christiansen, the process of crawling out of the early shock, numbness, grief, and blame did not follow any classical model of "grief recovery." Her "processing," as the professionals so impersonally put it, has been more a stew of various ingredients. "For me, it was not a matter of going through denial and then loss and then guilt and then anger. They all intertwine. There's no certain point where you can say, 'Now I am in recovery.' But there IS a progression over time.

"I can give you an idea of when my life quit being on hold and started to go forward and came into focus a little. We had been living right there in Hurst, right by the high school, Lori and I. We both got some counseling, not a lot, and it didn't do me much good because, I think, I didn't stay long enough or fully participate. I got more from Lori; we counseled each other, and worked through a lot of it.

"But I think it was about eight months later that both of us came to the full realization that our lives needed to start moving again, and we made the decision to move to Collin County. It was a decision to go forward. I wrote you the letter on about the first anniversary of his death, around Christmas. Back then those were black days and black times, and it's still not a great day—but dates and times and holidays become less meaningful in terms of focusing on loss.

"I have more of a day-to-day feeling of his presence that's there all the time. I miss him, but I have, I don't know, internal conversations with him at special times like that; a special connection with him at special times.

"There's no set, certain point in time, but eventually, blessedly, I guess, providentially, there is an overtaking of the memories that focus less on the death; the focus shifts back into the life. And when that takes over, the sweet memories come into play and become the stronger emphasis, and become more alive, and more real, and more a part of that life.

"As time goes on, as the memory of the death fades and the memory of the life increases, the importance of keeping that memory alive and well and nurtured becomes greater and greater. You become a caretaker for that memory. I took care of him when he was alive. And now, all I have to take care of is that memory."

The sweet moments, the sweet moments. Again and again she comes round to this phrase, and again and again I ponder exactly what it means to her.

Are the sweet moments merely the mental photographs she's using to assemble his internal scrapbook? Or the psychological bricks and stones and mortar for something bigger—his mental memorial? Or are the sweet moments the actual flesh and blood and food and oxygen she is using now to keep him alive inside of her now that he's gone—just as she did before he arrived?

Linda shows me a large color photograph of her son, taken a month or two before he shot himself. It's a large-format, studio shot. And, since the edges were blurred in the darkroom so that the face is most distinct, it's uncomfortably close to a photo of a ghost.

On looks alone, it is easy to see how he could get under a mother's skin in life and haunt her in death. It's a contradictory, compelling face.

Fierce, feral eyes flame out from a soft, cool-skinned, almost girlish face. Physically, he somehow calls to mind an artful cross between a hawk and a deer.

"Craig was very bright and sensitive; a lot of children that this (suicide) happens to are like that—sensitive, feeling, in touch, and full of feelings that are difficult for them to deal with. Of the three of my children, he was the most sensitive.

"And that sensitivity, of our having been so close and involved, was something I can still feel, almost like he's here, right now. His sister says she feels this, too. There are times when I wish I could touch base with him, talk to him, share with him like we used to. He was very articulate and the feelings and our relationship were intense. We were part of each other, whether physically together or not."

As both a lawyer and a mother, she came to admire her son's mind greatly. He wanted to follow in her footsteps, into the law. It was his idea, not hers (though she loved it). He had a future.

"He was not a drug addict or a gang member or another statistic. He was a bright child trying to become a man, with goals and aspirations and the risk of being overwhelmed by so many things. There isn't a 'standard' suicide, and I guess that's my point. He wasn't just a troubled youth to be stuck out there and labeled. He was many, many things, as is everyone.

"He was very much involved in this life. He and I would have discussions about God, and about whether or not there was a supreme being—about where the evidence is, what the meaning is. He brought up the subject of whether believing in the afterlife was something created by people just to make life here easier.

"Craig was a pragmatist, a realist. He had that scientific approach to what really is. He could separate what really is from what we merely thought things to be. He was much less a romantic than I, so I would say—I'm not saying he didn't believe in God, but he certainly questioned God's existence.

"The thing about the funeral fantasies—I don't think those were operational with him."

To some extent, Linda Christiansen's reaction is every mother's reaction, and her goal for Craig is every mother's. Even though her son is dead, she is still attempting to help him achieve immortality, and trying to get him all the allies she can find.

"Of course, it isn't just me. Craig, as is every child who leaves the world before his time, is also a son, a brother, a grandson, a nephew, a cousin, a friend, a classmate—many things to many people. And when he leaves this particular realm of his being, then that still exists; he is still all these things. If you leave this restaurant today and get killed by a truck tomorrow, you still exist for me.

"When I'm gone from this world, I will be remembered by grandchildren, just like I talk about my grandmother to my children who never knew her. I'm already sharing memories of Craig with his new little brother, whom he never knew. So his little brother knows him now through me.

"So the importance of Craig's life, and who he was and what he did and how he affected all of us will go on."

Some psychologists and others might characterize this keeping of Craig's life going on the inside as a refusal to let go, so I ask Linda if that's what it is.

"You bet it is. It most definitely is. And I don't have any reason to believe that I will ever reach the point of letting go. I don't know that I want to. If it became harmful to the other survivors, I might have trouble with it. But I don't have any evidence that it is harmful to them. I would never want to put them into the position of helping me carry on my own little psychosis.

"It's not a matter of dragging Craig along on every family outing for the benefit of good old Linda. I would never do that. It's more internal. I don't approach it with anyone until they approach it with me, not even with Lori. I have little pictures of Craig up around the house, but not an excessive number.

"I have a picture of me, Craig, and Lori in the living room. My little boy, when he was about three, wanted to know who that was with Mommy and Sister. I said, 'That's your brother. That's Craig.' And he wanted to know where Craig was. And because it's an easy, soft, uh, ha-ha cop-out kind of explanation that he could accept, I said, 'He's with Jesus.' And that's fine. He accepts that."

But that is not where Linda Christiansen believes that Craig is.

And so I asked, where does she believe he is?

And she smiled, touched her forehead, and left her finger there a long time.

"In here," she said.

Because of her openness and candor and grip on herself, idiosyncrasies and all, it did not seem inappropriate to ask to speak to him. I asked him what he would like to say; if there was any message he would like to impart.

I cannot report that Linda Christiansen's eyes changed color or her hairstyle changed or that her voice dropped an octave. There was, however, enough of a change in her cadence and her expression that some hairs on my arms stood up. And the ones on my neck joined them when I heard the tune Denny's Muzak system was playing over the background clank of cutlery: "Little Drummer Boy."

Here is what all of Craig Christiansen that is left in this world had to say:

"I feel so foolish. First of all, for putting myself in the condition where I lost control over what I was consciously able to do with my own life, because loss of control is something that I don't respect. It's something that I detest in myself. And I mourn the loss of the rest of my life, because I know intellectually that life sometimes has ups and down, but always has value: I know that.

"But most of all, I mourn for what happened to my survivors. Never, if I'd had a conscious thought of the intensity of pain that has been caused, would I ever have had this happen. I have never hurt man nor beast; I've always been a lover of life. And to see this kind of pain and this kind of loss and this devastation in the lives of so many people who cared about me and have lost me, is something that I would never consciously have happen.

"If I could do it all over, I would go all the way back to that first drink. I would get help, seek help, cry out for and demand help, even more than I already did. And I would make it right, if I could."

Linda Christiansen leans back a bit, and exhales, relaxes. She senses that nearly everything she has needed to say— and perhaps that Craig has needed to say—has been said.

"This has been hard for me," she says, "but I needed to do this. It is not enough to have a good life that has been more or less put back together. It is not enough that it's had a positive result—that I have a new appreciation for the ongoing miracle of life.

"I feel that, within whatever little bit of power I have to extend this beyond myself and the survivors and my little world, I have to reach out to people—people who may need to know that this can be ahead for them. If it would give them one minute of peace of mind a little sooner than they might otherwise have it, I've got to do it, hard as it is."

And then she sits a moment longer, physically and mentally preparing herself to stand up from the table and her past and walk out of Denny's, back into her life.

It is a pretty good life. A few years back she met a salt-of-the-earth type, a sheriff's deputy in Collin County, fell in love, and got married. He'd never had children, and wanted some. At the age of forty-two, still fit, she had Austin. He's five.

"As far as replacing Craig, it never struck me that way. It didn't have any meaning at all; you replace cars, not individuals. I was worried about the baby's health, at first, because of my age, and I worried how it would affect Lori. But remember, this was four or five years after Craig's death, and I had reached a point where I'd reconciled a lot of my feelings.

"There's a phrase from a poem, that goes: 'God gives us love; Something to love, he lends us.' God loaned me Craig for nineteen years. If I had a choice between not ever having had him, or having had him and going through all the pain of losing him, which would I take?

"I would take having him, and losing him. If I knew I was going to lose him in nineteen years, I would take him, on loan. And I felt the same way about my new child, Austin. If I only have him five minutes or seventy years, I gladly take him on loan. He doesn't really belong to me, and neither does Craig. I don't have the right to make the ultimate decision on how long or happy that life is going to be.

"I can just take that gift, and while it's in my hand, hold it, and if it leaves, let it go and keep the memory."

And so, almost on the anniversary of Craig's death,

she had Austin—a beautiful little blond-headed, active, loving, sensitive child—not unlike Craig in the basic qualities he brought to life.

"I don't know—are we given gifts like these to help us overcome our losses? Is it an extension of life to us from God, to give us a reason to accept both the losses and the memories of life? I'm a religious person, but only in how I feel. Maybe you can tell me. Maybe you have a closer connection."

For the life of me, I don't.

During the drive home this drizzly December day, I started to feel better about Linda's hanging on to Craig as though he were in some sense alive in her. In the restaurant, I'd been wondering how much room there was for Linda to really live with that much Craig in there.

But it works for her, makes her feel better. And in a heart that big, I expect there's plenty of room. I guess my highest hope for her would only be that there would come a day when she could put him aside if she wanted to.

But I also think about what else she'd said—that if I got killed by a truck, I would survive as a memory. And so I quit thinking about all this, and paid attention to the road. Survival like that I don't need just yet.

Chapter 12

I sometimes get as sick of talking about "suicide prevention" as most people do of hearing about it. And I've got a fairly elegant little two-part theory on that.

First is the very phrase, "suicide prevention," which sounds like a difficult if not impossible row to hoe. It sounds as if it belongs right up there on the feasibility scale with things like "ending all war" or "curing cancer in my lifetime."

Suicide has been with us always. It seems one of those almost insurmountable things that will admit no partial, incremental commitment. Suicide seems like one of those things we just have to live with.

I learned this the hard way, by batting my brains out against a huge wall during the production and distribution of my video, *Suicide Is Not Painless*.

And then I learned that the wall is really just an illusion.

That's the second part of the theory.

Of course, like any newborn and fiery-eyed crusader, I was hopelessly naive. I was reminded of this the other day when a woman called me and breathlessly said that she was just all of a sudden fiercely determined to do something about suicide. She felt designated by the finger of fate to follow in my footsteps and produce a video of her own, and she wanted some advice.

There was no problem with the money, she assured me, because she'd already raised it and was now ready to proceed, full speed ahead.

I asked her how much she'd raised.

"Almost fifteen hundred dollars," she said. I couldn't

help it: I just laughed. Because when I started mine, I thought that I could do it for about five thousand dollars.

I had stumbled onto the idea while somewhat frantically trying to find something, anything that would help the situation, and had been talking to a wide range of psychologists, survivors, school officials, and other ministers, but still was drawing a blank.

I was casually watching one of those Crimestopper things and—bingo! I thought, why not use a suicide re-enactment to save lives? I found a professional producer, Howard Englander, who told me that by cutting a lot of corners and scrimping and saving, he could keep the combined production and distribution costs to around sixty-five thousand dollars. Of course my jaw hit the floor. But after it came back up to my face and I had some time to think about it, I decided I would do it. The next step was raising the money, because I sure didn't have it.

I've never been a good fund-raiser, but I had to try. I talked to churches, civic clubs, business and law enforcement people who were aware of the problem and wanted to help.

I remember that the father of one of the two boys out there in that pickup by that sad and lonely hill had suffered a stroke, and was in the hospital. The nurses on the floor were taking up a collection for the video. He heard about it, and though hard-pressed, was among the first to contribute, an amount of $37.50.

By February of 1986, I had exceeded my own expectations by raising thirty-two thousand dollars, and we were ready to begin.

That first day of shooting kind of gave me a chill. There was something very real about it. I knew it was a video, but setting it up—the story and character were a composite of the cases I had seen to date—made all the cases come together, all of them seeming solid and forbidding. We shot it on the shores of Lake Arlington, slow waves lapping dolefully at shore, a cold February sun setting in the background, and a seventeen-year-old boy slumped over the wheel of his car at the edge of the water.

The screenplay, written by Marc Bockmon, aimed at dramatizing the fact that suicide is a permanent solution to a temporary problem. That one image—the winter sun, the lonely, battered car—seemed to sum it up for me.

And I think it did for the rest of the cast, too.

Howard Englander raced home one evening to his daughter, just to talk, just to be sure that he was truly listening to what she said—to make sure that he knew her, and knew her mind. Matt Holbein, who played the victim in the film, the young hopeless man slumped over the wheel, later said that the role had helped him cherish life more than ever.

"I feel so sorry for my character, who has lost total motivation for life. It horrifies me that I'm the same age as people who are doing this to themselves. It's more than a job; I feel I may really help somebody. I don't know who, but I am sure it will help someone."

The video lasts twenty-two minutes and follows a teenager through suicide, showing how he feels and the effect his death has on his mother, father, younger sister, and friend. The danger signs of suicide are discussed and the importance of listening, really listening, to teenagers is stressed, as is the necessity to get them professional help when they need it.

And with it finally in the can, I set out to conquer the world.

And, of course, didn't.

The video has gotten a very positive response from those who have seen it. It even won fifth place among twelve hundred entries in the New York Film Festival. I know it has saved lives over the years since its production.

I thought it would be a perfect tool for schools. I thought we would need two companies just to duplicate the tapes for all those who would want it. But some are scared of it. Many schools said "Well, our psychologists test for this, and, as you know, we're in a kind of a financial crunch. And we're really, well, we're kind of scared that if we show your film and then some kid commits suicide, well, we'd be liable."

Of course, that was not the reaction in every school district; the ones that have used it have gotten a lot of good out of it. But what is disturbing is the apathy that surrounds the subject, the unwillingness to address it.

I experienced this when I was in San Antonio for a speaking engagement. I read in the paper that they were being plagued with a rash of youth suicides, and that city leaders had pulled together a blue-ribbon panel to talk about the problem. A doctor, whose name was mentioned prominently in the article, was among them. So I picked up the telephone in my hotel room and called this doctor's office. I didn't get through to him, but talked at some length to his secretary, telling her who I was and why I'd called. I told her about the program we had introduced in Arlington, and how we'd gone from six teen suicides in one year—and an average of three—to zero teen suicides, two years in a row.

I added: "I don't want you to think for one moment that I am hawking this film. I don't get any money from it. I am not pushing the video, but I am trying to help. So if you'll have the doctor contact me, I'll mail you a video free of charge. Just have him call me if he's interested, and I'll send it to you."

I haven't heard from him yet.

This happened to an administrator in the Arlington school system, also, when he responded to the news that three teenagers had killed themselves in the course of one week in the small town of Sheridan, Arkansas. He called me saying he wanted to write to the folks in Sheridan explaining our program. He wanted to tell them about the video, and, with my permission, would tell them that if their little school district couldn't afford it, we'd be more than happy to send them a free copy.

I agreed. He wrote the letter, a nice one, and mailed it. He sent me a copy of it. We're both still waiting for a response.

To overcome such apathy, I thought I would approach churches, which would surely want to do something to prevent suicide. Although many bought it, even more did not.

A disturbing but revealing event involved a nephew of mine who was thrilled about the video. He was in a coffee shop telling some friends about it, and what we hoped to do with it. Among the group was a man who was with his pastor. The man said, "Wow, that's great," when he heard about the video, and asked my nephew how much it cost. (We were selling it for $149.) Then he turned to his minister and said, "You know, we really need this for the church."

The pastor said: "We can't afford it."

A week later, the man killed himself.

The next time the preacher was in the coffee shop, he told the others, with great sadness: "His life wasn't worth $149 to us."

When I tell that story to groups I always think that it will motivate them to get the video. But it doesn't, because people don't ever think it's going to happen to them. Even when the odds are very, very good that it is. One example of this was a woman who called me. She lived in nearby Grapevine and said she'd heard about my work, and had called me because she was afraid her son might be suicidal. She told me more about him, and she had good reason for her fears. Her son was one troubled fourteen-year-old. If anybody was ever suicidal, it was he.

So I told her: "Listen, ma'am, tonight I'm going to be speaking on suicide at the high school auditorium in your city. When I finish speaking, if you'll just come up and identify yourself, I'll work with you to do whatever needs to be done to save the life of your son."

She said: "Oh, I knew you were going to be here, but I'm sorry, I just won't be able to be there. We have a dinner engagement."

And so, as the eighties turned to the nineties, I found that I too was becoming very weary of suicide prevention.

I had been living it since 1984. And that's a long time to go on and on repeating the same information on the same subject two and three nights a week.

Suicide is a deadly subject, in more than one way. In casual conversation, the subject is dismissed as morbid—and in many respects it is. It's like suggesting that you go shopping for burial plots. But more than that, there's that sense of total apathy—of denial—surrounding the subject. It's rooted in the belief that it always happens to *other* families.

In fact, hanging on to this belief is the way people protect themselves from their own subverted fears of suicide. They maintain the belief that something is wrong with "those" folks, while nothing's wrong with them.

"My kids are not on drugs. Well, not very much; and my kids are not drinking. Well, not very much. And they don't seem very depressed, much; and when they are depressed they seem to handle it pretty well; they just go on up to their rooms. I don't think we have a problem with suicide at my house."

It's the same with many churches. If you start trying to talk suicide prevention, you'll often find that the key people in the church all believe that there is no problem in their church. They don't have anybody who's suicidal, and if they're not bothered with the problem, why would they want to talk about it?

Yes, I found myself getting tired of it.

When I first started out, I would hear someone say, "Chaplain Elliott, I have tried to commit suicide three times."

After I started doing radio and television talk shows at the rate of at least one a week, four to five hours a month, I would hear people say, "I've tried to kill myself five times." And I began having some real changes in my emotions.

I wanted to say, "Well, if you've tried five times, something's wrong. You are either flat-out lying, or you are just really dumb, because out of five tries, surely one would have worked. What I think you really did was make five dramatic gestures."

And then one day, for no particular reason, just sort of out of a bright blue sky, it hit me—what I was doing wrong, thinking wrong, and why people in general just plain **hate** to talk about suicide prevention.

Suicide isn't the problem at all. Suicide, when all is said and done, is not a disease. It is instead only a complication of a disease, a symptom—albeit a serious one—that is mistaken by the sufferer for a cure.

The disease—the real problem—is misery.

So now I don't think of the process as being "suicide prevention" but rather as "misery reduction." And that's a more manageable task. We know how to look for someone who's miserable.

Most of the sources of misery come under the heading of stress. We all face stress, of course; it is when we are no longer able to cope with it that it becomes truly misery-making to the extent that it is life-threatening. Included among the signs that one is losing the resiliency, equilibrium, and perspective needed for coping is helplessness. The person is (or believes he is) no longer able to handle events; he feels he has exhausted all options to handle the situation facing him. He is miserable. If the next step—that of hopelessness—enters the picture, he is truly "at risk." His reasoning is in fact impaired, and tells him that every possible avenue of coping leads to a negative conclusion.

What kind of general situation can lead to the kind of stress that, in a reasonably "normal" adult, could bring about this sense of helpless hopelessness? It varies, of course. However, there are some general categories of events and circumstances which induce these extremes of misery.

Loss of a relationship. Death, divorce, desertion, even relocation are all highly stressful events. No loss of relationship (particularly with children or adolescents) should be taken lightly.

A major blow to the ego. Unemployment, when it results in a significant blow to self-esteem, fits this category, as would failure in school or a loss in business, unwelcome retirement, or any major unwelcome change in status.

The two factors are, of course, closely intertwined. The loss of a relationship, especially a romantic one through divorce or breakup, can be a major blow to your ego. Your perception of yourself is, to some extent—and the less, the better—dictated by estimates of how others feel about you. Many losses, whether of relationships or employment (which is, after all, another relationship), often change the reflection you see in the mirror.

Coping, then, is a matter of deciding how to deal with that mirror image: to change your behavior for the better; to decide that the disapproving person is wrong; or to let your opinion of yourself become negative. It is this last course of action, followed to its extreme, that may lead someone to suicide.

There are many external signs when someone is struggling with the treadmill of depression. Among them are the following:

An appearance of depression—looking haggard, poorly focused, slack-faced.

Withdrawal. The classical case of this is someone who is constantly fatigued and retreats for long periods of time to his home or his room to sleep for far longer than normal. Lesser withdrawals may be from friends and family or activities. You shouldn't panic at the first sign of withdrawal, of course; we all need periods of it occasionally; but if it lasts days and then weeks, there is cause for alarm.

Mood swings. Everybody has good days and bad. But if the changes and the range become dramatic, closer scrutiny may be needed.

Changes in sleeping habits, whether too much or too little. A person's fascination with the amount of sleep he has had may also be a sign.

Decline in sexual vigor or interest.

Increased or immoderate alcohol abuse.

Languor—the loss of ambition, interest, energy, and ability to concentrate. This last may manifest itself outwardly as an intense concentration on something that is actually an escape from reality—compulsive and uncharacteristic fiddling or puttering, for example. This may most clearly reveal itself in poor work performance.

Unusual self-deprecation. This may indicate feelings of hopelessness or remorse.

If the treadmill of depression runs long enough and hard enough, finally, the victim, hopeless and exhausted, wants only to get off, and may not care how.

So of course there is sometimes a catch to this "misery reduction" thing. Somewhere between your learning of their misery and your getting them to the place where it can gradually be reduced, your patient might kill himself.

If the person begins to appear fascinated with death, talks about suicide, gives away important possessions or shows other signs of resignation, you should begin to tackle the question of whether he's actually thinking of suicide. Some approaches in dealing with this question are better than others.

First, make it clear which of his behaviors have caused you concern, and ask him to help you understand what is going on. Listen carefully. If the answers heighten your concern, ask him, as tactfully as possible, whether he has been considering some kind of harm to himself (the language you use depends on your relationship). Do not allow a joking reply or a hostile reaction to back you down. Pursue it gently but firmly, expressing your concern and restating the question along the lines of: "I'm really not kidding. You seem so down that I really have been wondering if you've been considering suicide as a possibility. Have you?"

From there, his answer may take you one of three ways.

If he persists in denying that he is suicidal, you might drop it for the moment and bring it up at a later time, or express your fears to others close to him. You can't force anyone to admit that they're thinking about suicide. (But remember, a denial does not mean that he is "in denial.") No may simply mean No. It may be that, while he is not at his best, he has not been considering suicide. You may wish to make an arrangement with him, getting him to firmly promise that if things ever do reach a stage where suicide is an option, that he will talk with you.

If he admits to such feelings, however, it is important that you discover the intended method. If he says that he has not thought about it, the risk may not be as great. You will still need to help him focus on the problems he is facing and find out what troubles suicide seems to offer surcease from. However, if he has thought about a method, he is in deep trouble. If the plan is strange and unconventional, he may be showing signs of psychosis, and require immediate medical attention. If the plan is more conventional, remember that the more concise the plan, the more likely the event.

Next, determine the availability of the method he's thinking of using. If he's thinking about killing himself with a gun, does he own one? Where is it? If it's on the premises or readily available, the risk is further increased. If he has motive, method, opportunity, and, in your judgment, seems just disturbed enough to do it, help him to see that he needs some professional help.

Some psychologists feel that the difference between a suicidal and a non-suicidal person in the face of a similar amount of stress lies in the background of the person in question.

The person who is believed to be a higher risk is the one who is chronically unable to maintain warm, mutual relationships throughout his life. He is unable to express his need for others—and this in spite of the fact that his need may be stronger than that of non-suicidal people.

His problems mount, thanks to the fact that, because he cannot express his needs, they are seldom gratified, adding to his misery and frustration. Further, even when others make a special effort to be helpful and supportive, he tends to either withdraw from the relationship, deny that help is in fact being offered—or at the least, distrust motives. In fact, he expects negative feelings from others and, because this attitude results in a measure of churlishness, he frequently gets them.

Here is the saddest of cases, of course: The one that

you and society at large are likely to miss. He has locked out the world, and has learned to mask his misery.

You won't find out about him unless you just happen to stumble over him.

It's because of the way he is.

But he was not always so.

And that is cause for hope.

Perhaps the best thing we can hope to do for both "misery reduction" and suicide prevention is to help them while they're still young enough to change.

Chapter 13

Traditional wisdom says that before someone kills himself, he issues a cry for help, and that is to a large extent true. In fact, we should pay very close attention to a young person who overtly asks for help. Since adolescents are usually trying—almost obsessively—to prove their independence and self-possession, a request for help from a teenager is a strong cry for help.

But the conventional wisdom, applied too broadly and arbitrarily, can become an onerous and unnecessary burden on survivors, particularly in the case of youth suicide. Survivors feel they should have known, should have seen some clue, should have done something, if only they'd paid more attention...

This endless loop of questions tortures survivors of suicide. But the truth is often that they shouldn't have known, couldn't have known. While the suicide may indeed have cried for help, it may not have been directed at the survivor who is agonizing about it.

Of course, in the case of the truly determined and unambivalently self-destructive suicide, the cover of secrecy, and, maliciously, maintaining the element of surprise for the survivors can become all-important. In such a case, nobody could have known because the suicide wanted *nobody* to know.

A "loner" is equally hard to read, and nearly three-fourths of adolescents who attempt suicide fall into this category. While some come from families in which their parents also suffer low self-esteem, most come from relatively "normal" parents. Nonetheless, loners—those

with little or no social contact with others—are at great
risk for suicide because they have been taught, perhaps
inadvertently, to avoid expressing their feelings. So they
give no signs of their depressed or desperate outlook.

There are reasons for the loneliness and loner-liness,
but in cases where the deed is already done, the reasons,
often obscure, die with them.

It is therefore pointless for a survivor to ask for the rest
of their life how they could have missed the signs. Maybe
there weren't any; maybe the changes occurred so
suddenly, so secretly and over so "little" that it would
have eluded all but a mind reader.

Parents of some suicides are tortured by the thought
that maybe they were too hard on the child. Well, maybe.
But also, maybe not. More than a third of all teen suicides
may be in response to a disciplinary crisis—not, however,
after one, but rather in *anticipation* of one. Knowing he is
about to be caught in some kind of serious trouble, a teen
trying to figure out exactly what the consequences of his
actions will be, experiences great uncertainty. To avoid it,
he passes both judgment and punishment on himself.
And the punishment is the death penalty.

The parent may be left forever in the dark about the
"crime" the teen committed and the punishment he feared.

Further, the odds are almost equally good that the
suicide may have had *nothing* to do with the quality of
home life—more than a fifth come purely as a result of a
loss of face with peers. Then there are the "impulsive"
suicides—where, faced with a difficult but not
overwhelming situation, a teenager whimsically imagines
suicide as a solution, and then, because of poor impulse
control, follows the whim. Many of the people who survive
these "impetuous" attempts claim never to have
considered it until the moment of the attempt. Though
the claim in itself is suspect, as there are probably deeper
subconscious causes, it can be argued that such impulsives
would have issued no clear-cut "cry for help."

Nevertheless, some signs may be there—and in a society
where a young person tries to kill himself and another

one succeeds every ninety minutes, being able to recognize the signs and precursors could well save a life.

Our task is to see the signs or cries for help if indeed they occur. And if they do, your duty and your responsibilities are much more clear-cut. Some friends and family fail to intervene because of the dangerously modern and sometimes deadly rationale that they are not experts, and so should not try to handle it. (Trust me: If you ever have to live through a suicide, you will probably spend the rest of your life becoming an expert. Suicide survivors become compulsive "experts.")

In matters of suicide intervention, something almost always beats nothing. It is one thing not to know it was coming and thus fail to prevent it, and quite another to suspect it but neglect it. (One of the strangest and most disturbingly dismissive comments I ever heard came from a mother whose daughter had killed herself a couple of years earlier: "We knew she wasn't happy—but she never would have been happy even if she hadn't killed herself." Here is a woman subconsciously screaming at the top of her lungs, "Not my fault, not my fault, she just wasn't happy!")

The rules that apply to the dire task of detecting and then preventing a youthful suicide are the same rules that apply to simple good parenting. Following them as a general rule also addresses a host of lesser troubles, and could well result in an offspring who would never for a moment consider self-destruction; following them could result in a healthy, happy, well-balanced adult.

The extent to which you have a good working relationship with your child is also the extent to which you will be able to see the potentially more dangerous signs of suicide, should they arise. Perhaps, then, the best all-round general preventative is simple communication. But before there can be communication, there must be understanding. This is not merely a matter of having an "understanding attitude," nodding at the appropriate moment and making smiling sympathetic sounds and then congratulating yourself on how understanding you are. While some recommend "two-way" communication,

I think it's more accurate to say that it calls for 1 1/2-way communication: They mostly talk, you mostly listen. You ask questions and listen some more.

Before you can help, you have to know what is REALLY going on. And before you can know that, you must earn— not demand—their trust and make them realize that you are not preparing to judge their statements or beliefs, but only to befriend and help them.

You must have a true understanding with them, an understanding based in two realities.

The first is yours. Where are you with this kid? Who are you to this kid? And is that where you need to be? On this point, kidding yourself could be fatal.

You have no doubt heard the news that the American family has taken a beating in recent years as it has stripped itself of extended relationships. Now it's often just mom, dad, kids. In many instances it has stripped itself down a further step, to either a mom—or, less likely, a dad—and some kids.

If not gone completely, then certainly quite distant are the once-close aunts, uncles, cousins, in-laws, and grandparents of yesteryear who took up some of the burden of child-rearing and moral education. And, though it would seem that a smaller, more nuclear family would also be closer and more self-sufficient, that is often not the case. Increasingly, parents have delegated (some might say abdicated from) their responsibility for ethics, education, spiritual guidance, health, and psychological well-being to unconcerned others—paid professionals in government, education and the criminal justice system.

With this transfer of responsibility comes an all-too-convenient excuse to shift blame. Where once parents assumed responsibility for their offspring and were motivated at least in part to meet these responsibilities from fear of being perceived as a failure, now many parents are little more than advocates and apologists for their sons and daughters, blaming the educational system, socio-economic injustice, television, movies, and anything else they can think of.

The point here is you've got to take responsibility for your child, or "understanding" becomes a matter of pointless and conspiratorial sympathizing and validating excuses in an already over-excused and finger-pointing society. Because while the changes in the American family are serious and far-reaching, the most important factor in a child's ability to overcome damage from all the negatives—the loss of the extended family, divorce, social pressures, and economic woes—still remains a positive relationship with the remaining parent.

The second reality is yours also. Before understanding your child, you must understand yourself. If you are too tired, too busy, too absorbed in your own problems, overcome it. Make time—and don't begrudge the time or aggrandize yourself for having given it; it's the least you can do.

If you're emotionally blocked, a loner, or depressed, get help. You may be dragging your child down with you. Parents who are themselves depressed tend to rear children who are—statistics show—themselves clinically depressed.

Once you are clear on who and where you are as a parent, determine where your child is—learn his world and his reality, and the peculiarities of those realities facing young people of junior high and high school age.

It is all too easy for older people, having slowly watched in themselves the waning of the energy they felt in their youth, both to envy the young their vigor and to fail to remember and thus to empathize with those travails that derive precisely from that overabundance of mental and physical energy. As adults, we have a tendency to brush aside the unhappiness of young people. It must be remembered that the energy of young people, because of their lack of experience, is a lot more like nitroglycerine than a steady strong and useful electrical current. It is unstable, unpredictable, difficult to handle, and hard to efficiently direct. This wild raw energy is, in many respects, a liability as much as a blessing, and a source of problems rather than a solution.

Adolescence is a fractious and frightful time at best, and the educational institutions of society—almost always shaped by the attitudes of those who have forgotten—sometimes only exacerbate an already-bad situation.

To understand, you need to know (if not remember) the psychological and social pressures that come with puberty.

For the precocious, the early teens may be a wonderful opportunity for expanding social contacts and entering joyously into a larger world. But for the large majority of the rest of adolescents, the gangly, the pimply, the "still carrying some baby fat," the shy and the uncertain—in short, most kids—school can seem like nothing more than the place where they are daily thrown to the mercy of their rather merciless peers. For many, school is no fun at all.

(It is hardest, perhaps, for parents who were at the top of the heap during their own adolescence to empathize with their own children as they go through this phase. Worse, many such parents saddle their offspring with the unreasonable expectation that they will be "just like I was.")

It is in school, particularly junior high, that some young people first encounter racism and "looks-ism." It is here that many get their first dose of cruel competition, lack of understanding, and unreasonable expectations. It is also here, where students continue to be arbitrarily grouped by chronological age rather than actual levels of development, that many may first begin to feel that they don't fit in.

And the truth may well be that they do not fit in with the rest of their group. While all first-graders are more or less equal, the same cannot be said for junior high and high-schoolers. A person may safely be counted upon to turn thirteen years old exactly 4,748 days after one is born, but truly God only knows when puberty will hit. And whether it hits early or late may have as profound an impact, positive or negative, as anything else that will ever happen to the child. Children between the ages of twelve and fifteen are probably the least understood segment of the population. Parents may regard these years and these changes with wry bemusement, harking vaguely back through the rose-colored glasses of hindsight to their own pubescence. We tend to forget the unpleasant, and the truth in many cases is that the onset of puberty is fraught with far more than the mere physiological and hormonal changes most adults remember or mis-remember.

Studies have shown that, almost as important as puberty itself is the question of when in the child's life it begins—early or late. This factor may be crucial in the development of the young person's self-esteem, personal identity, and even his successful competition in school. For example, early onset is a distinct advantage for boys and a disadvantage for girls. Early-blooming boys are seen as more popular by their peers; they excel in sports and, frequently, academics. They are thus given more leadership (read "power") roles by adults, who sometimes see them as simply more attractive. As a result, they are frequently more self-confident and independent—and, by inference, less prone to suicide—than their late-maturing peers, who are often found to have less self-esteem and more unconstructive rebelliousness, who harbor stronger feelings of rejection by their peers and suffer from them more.

Further, in terms of learning to deal with members of the opposite sex, the late-bloomer has to start from behind. He has a harder time learning to get along and may bring a certain desperation to his search.

For girls, the situation is reversed. Early-pubescing girls often feel out of place among their less well-developed peers, and sometimes develop the kind of submissive social behavior that is characteristic of low self-esteem.

You also need to better understand what may seem like a desperate need for approval by the child's peers. Some parents view with distaste and distrust the young teenager's fascination with "popularity" and being "in," dismissing it as an unwholesome and unnecessary obsession, and may automatically perceive the peer group the child is courting as "the enemy." This can cause problems, because although while the wrong peer group may indeed handicap a teenager's development, the parents themselves may unintentionally force their children into such groups by distrusting their children's ability to choose their own friends.

The simple truth is, of course, that the adolescent, lacking any means of measuring the new and profound changes taking place in his life and emotions, is simply seeking to ascertain, through broader social contacts, that he is in fact normal. And the junior high school environment may be one of the worst in which to seek such assurance.

The gradation system—elementary, junior high and high school—was designed to gradually ease the child from the self-contained, one-teacher, day-long classroom to the wider and more mobile world of high school. Even in an almost-perfect world, imposing these social changes on a young person at the same time as profound physical and psychological changes are occurring would seem rather severe. In reality, many schools, particularly the rough-and-tumble inner city schools, are little more than places where young, unformed minds are thrown to other unformed minds. Many are places where intellectual and scholastic achievement are officially rewarded by administrators against an opposing sub-text of disapproval from the kids.

In this environment the pressures may combine to produce someone whose staunchest hope is that he will be perceived as decidedly average. The hardships imposed by the lack of a fully developed, fully centered, and grounded personality are only complicated by the fact that it is here, in school, that one first encounters and is forced to incorporate external and arbitrary value systems; here, before he has learned who he is, he is coerced and conditioned into measuring himself by equally external and arbitrary yardsticks of achievement and worth. Since the young mind deals in labels more readily than logic, it is all too ready to translate these labels into definitions of self-worth. And a brilliant poet or a potential Mark Twain may remain asleep or even die—if grades and the teacher's approval become integrated into his view of himself—in a young person who cannot for the life of him master the art of diagramming a sentence.

In only slightly better psychological shape is the young person who is beginning to know his own value and abilities but who goes unrecognized by the system. He may fall prey to feelings of alienation, of being Brilliant and Misunderstood.

Consider your own high school reunions, ten, twenty or thirty years after commencement; it is often incredible to you that the well-dressed, polished man who has returned after making a huge killing in real estate or at the forefront of computer technology is the same hopeless, faceless guy who lurked in the lockers and made a mess of business math. Your own amazement is proof of the internalization of those judgments made by the system and by peer groups long ago.

Yet many parents have given the responsibility for evaluating their children to these systems. It may be that the best thing you can do for a child is let him know that, while school is very important, the judgments made by the system and peers are not the only criteria by which he will be judged, nor are they the only predictors of his ultimate failure or success.

Remember that the kid you see leaving for school in the morning and coming home in the afternoon may have gone through pure misery in between. And while it seems a tempest in a teapot to you, that is only because you have lived long enough to put it far behind you. But it is still his only world—the larger one beyond family, friends, and childish fun into which you have told him he has no choice but to grow.

In the truest sense, his ability to negotiate these years may mean the difference between life or death, sooner or later. Because the seeds of most adult suicides are sown in these formative years.

Kids want discipline and guidance. It is important for you to realize, however, that there is a great difference between true guidance and mere pronouncements. In fact, arbitrary pronouncements, maybe even your own, may be part of the problem. It may be that the rules that society seems to be asking him to abide by are unreasonable, or that the reasons are not understood by him, and are thus perceived as hostile.

In homes where parents are rigidly authoritarian and require unquestioned obedience from the child in all things, depression may be the result. The adolescent in such an environment has no opportunity to postulate and then test his own ideals, values and morals—which is necessary before a healthy separation from parents can begin. The other problem is that authoritarian parents play too directly to the kind of either/or, no-way-out thinking, the inability to see anything beyond the current pain or fear, that characterizes suicide.

Perhaps equally as risky are those environments in which the parents assume a hands-off, anything-goes attitude toward guidance. By refusing to guide, intervene or interfere under any circumstances, such parents fail to set limits, leaving the teenager upset and bewildered. When a young person experiences autonomy—his natural goal at this point—with so small an effort, he may question its validity, and continue to act ever more wildly, testing it for some response.

Apparently the best is somewhere in between. The lowest incidence of teenage depression seems to arise in homes where there are some rules and guidelines, but where these are the result of input and open communication between all members of the family.

Adolescents are both extremists and extremely egocentric. In favorable circumstances, when things are good, this extreme, center-of-the-universe way of viewing the world creates those wonderful, sepia-toned memories that may last a lifetime—of first kisses that seemed to last all night, of first loves that were certain to last a lifetime; of good friends and high adventures that seemed to foretell magical majestic futures unfolding. These intense highs are somewhat more muted for adults. The man who just got the promotion and the big raise may feel great joy and even shout and click his heels—but somewhere in the back of his mind he knows that a year from now, it'll just be a job, just what he does for a living. He knows that the brand-new car will, some few thousand miles down the road, start to make a funny noise.

On the flip side are the negative feelings. To an adult, the feelings engendered by failing the civil service exam or losing a girl or wrecking a car are unpleasant—but he knows they will pass; teenagers, on the other hand, have a tendency to see each misery as complete and extending from the present into "forever." Where an adult might be tempted to mildly rebuke himself—I should've tried harder—the more extreme adolescent faced with failure may say things ranging all the way from "I'm worthless," to "I hate myself," to "I am the worst person in the world," and then to "I do not deserve to live."

Most of us, having survived adolescence, have also survived many such moments of "unending" misery and humiliation; it was through these moments, in fact, that we learned to put "unending" in quotation marks.

Perhaps the simplest definition of our task as adults, then, is to be able to monitor young people to find out which crises are moving them closer to an adult awareness of those quotations marks, and which crises may seem so large that they require intervention and guidance.

The most important thing, when dealing with someone in trouble or emotional stress, is not that you can say something to them that might be helpful, but that you can listen to them. Nothing you can say can heal them; but something they might say to you could help them begin to heal themselves.

Your end of the conversation is most helpful when it only encourages them to talk more, to think about what they are saying—and shows that you clearly understand. You do not have to be a professional to be helpful to someone who is having the kind of trouble that could lead to a suicide—or to someone who is a survivor in the aftermath of one. You just have to listen and know a few common-sense rules of thumb.

First, it is not your job to fix things for other people: You don't have to have all the answers; they have to find answers for themselves, because those are the ones that will do them the most good.

Further, the answers may change over time, and you should let them—in fact, that is what you're after. A person's viewpoints and opinions may privately strike you as way off the mark. Give them credit for having sense enough to correct themselves as time goes by; your job is to help them help themselves.

There are certain things that will help you be a good listener:

1. Be there. Be in present time, and in the present space. If you are thinking about tomorrow's activities or replaying yesterday's failures, you are elsewhere—and to the extent you are not there with the person in trouble, he is alone.

2. Bring to the table a sincere listening attitude. Listening requires genuine interest in learning how the other person really feels, and freedom from suppositions about how they should feel.

3. If you don't "get it," say so. Listening requires you, the listener, to genuinely pay attention to the other person's thoughts and not get lost in your own.

4. Don't hide your own feelings as you listen. Some people feel that non-judgmental and objective listening means that you must look and act inscrutable. If people wanted that, they'd be as well off addressing the doorknob. Your job in listening is to be human, and being human means reacting. If what they say makes you sad, say so. And if they are feeling better, rejoice with them. The main thing to remember about reacting, however, is you are not trying to express yourself so much as help the person further his own thinking.

5. This is not about you. It is not for your benefit. You are not looking for thanks or admiration or recognition. You are not even after the warm and fuzzy feeling you get when you make someone feel better. You are trying

to help someone go through thoughts and feelings and hopefully get to new thoughts and feelings. The only thanks you may get is your own realization that such may have occurred.

6. Be patient. You are helping someone to deal with things that are overwhelming—otherwise the person would not be having a serious problem. You may cover the same topic over and over again as insights progress.

Chapter 14

"I'll bet you saw lots of people killed on television," said the boy. "Thousands of them," said the old-timer. "The real killings went on at dinner time during the news shows, then afterward they'd taper off with a few make-believe killings to get everybody's mind soothed down." "Those must have been the days," said the boy.—A Heap of Seeing, from *So This Is Depravity*, by Russell Baker

Every once in a while I find myself wondering: Who counsels the counselors? Who debriefs the debriefers? We all have our flashbacks—our mental tapes that play unbidden over and over again. There is something about moments of bare and unadulterated horror that works on the human spirit to make a permanent etching. No effort at all is required to make these terrible tapes rewind and play, rewind and play—in full stereo, technicolor, high fidelity and Sensurround.

I am sometimes startled purely by how clearly certain moments come back to me.

Thomas Edward Stephens is standing there in front of the convenience store, pistol held about waist-high. He slowly lowers it, lower, lower, lower... until the gun is pointing at the pavement.

As I and the rest of the officers on the scene breathe a collective sigh of relief, he almost casually raises it to the side of his head and—boom—pulls the trigger.

Unforgettable enough, at that point. But what glues it deep into my memory is my amazement and revulsion at the fact that, as he collapsed to the pavement and quickly died in a spreading pool of blood, a crowd soon gathered outside the police line to view the deadly scene. One man even held up his son so the boy could see.

Once upon a time I had reserved judgment on the question so often asked of me: Is there such a thing as a good suicide? There had been some that had truly moved me, some with which I could truly sympathize.

One which has stayed with me over the years was that of Anna H.

It was in 1991. One of our dispatchers picked up the phone, and an older woman on the other end, sounding very calm, collected, deliberate, told the dispatcher that she had just shot and killed her ill husband, and that, when she finished talking to the dispatcher, she was going to do the same to herself.

The dispatcher tried to keep the woman on the line, trying to talk her out of it and buying some time.

But the woman wouldn't have any of it. She gave her daughter's name and address, and her own name and address. And, with the dispatcher still trying to get her to talk about it, she said goodbye and hung up the phone.

By the time we got there, it was all over. Completely.

She had taken care of everything. She'd left a short note, with her will lying next to it.

It was dark in that bedroom, in that modestly comfortable home. They were both in bed. She had apparently shot him, then gotten out of bed and made her call to the police department.

Then she must have gotten back in bed and shot herself.

The thing that I couldn't help but notice, and the thing that sealed the scene into my memory, was that, in that dimness, if you didn't look too closely, it was a scene of great love.

There lay a man and a woman who'd been together well over fifty years. From all the accounts, she was a kind and gentle lady, someone, as the oft-repeated cliche goes, who "would never do something like that."

He was ill and getting progressively worse. People who live with someone in the worst extremes of certain diseases tell you that it gets very lonely. The person who was once your constant companion, your friend for life, can become a burden.

It was easy to see that she'd done it out of love. She couldn't bear to be alone, but couldn't bear to have him placed in a home. As she had told the dispatcher, she'd thought about it for a long time, and had decided this was the way to go.

She had taken one other step to make the ending as final and as painless as possible: to make sure that her daughter wouldn't stumble in unawares and find her parents that way. She had called the police.

This is as close as I've ever come to a "good" suicide—but it was only "close." Because there was still the daughter. And it fell to me to tell her, as gently as possible. I told her about the scene, about my feelings about it—that in spite of the great tragedy, it also seemed to reflect great love.

I don't know how much comfort that afforded her. It's very difficult to soften the news when the news is as bad as this. Great love or not, the mother didn't have to live with the decision. The daughter, who didn't get a vote, carries it with her forever.

With the clear-eyed acuity accorded by hindsight, perhaps it is understandable that the crowd gathered when Thomas Stephens shot himself on the sidewalk outside the convenience store; from their limited perspective, he was a very bad man. And maybe there was no other way for it all to have ended.

After all, he had done a very bad thing. He'd killed one clerk, the mother of three, and wounded another while holding as hostage his estranged wife, who was also a clerk there.

It had been a six-hour ordeal for the Arlington Police Department, providing the kind of situation that every tactical-section commander has nightmares about. Stephens had entered the store about noon in a drunken rage. He then pulled his weapon and about a half-dozen customers made a hasty exit. Seconds later, the shooting began. Terri Palmer, thirty, with whom Stephens' wife and two teenaged children were living while Mrs. Stephens waited for her divorce, probably died instantly. The other store employee, Craig Talley, lay on the floor with gunshot wounds to his arm, leg, and foot.

Several alternate plans had been initiated and aborted throughout the cold and seemingly unending afternoon as officers racked their brains for a means of ending the situation without further loss of life.

SWAT teams have been glorified by the media in recent years; in their case, the hype matches the reality. They deserve the glory. Not only do they make life or death decisions, but they also put their lives on the line in implementing those decisions.

Negotiations with Stephens were going nowhere, although at one point about four hours into the siege he allowed officers to come into the store to remove the two victims. Stephens continued to drink beer from the cooler, and was becoming increasing belligerent and profane.

The simplest and most expedient solution—simply letting APD sharpshooters "take him out"—had been ruled out because of Stephens' and his wife's location. He was keeping her to the rear of the store and that left a lot of trajectory-altering glass and shelving between the rifles and him.

At one point, the plan was to put two officers into one of the department's reinforced Suburbans and have them drive it, full-speed, through the brick skirting and plate glass at the front of the store. Then, it was hoped, they would be able to jump out of the truck and save the woman—opening fire on Stephens if necessary.

And it was felt that it would be very necessary.

There's no other way to put it: The men volunteering for that mission—going up against an enraged drunk with a .357 magnum which he'd had no hesitation about using—had to face the fact that they just might be about to die.

The first one came over to me with his cap. Since he was going to be wearing a protective steel mask along with his flak jacket, he wouldn't be wearing his cap. He handed it to me, and then reached over and squeezed my hand. He said, "Think about me." He didn't say pray for me; he said, "Think about me."

The second handed me his sunglasses. He said, "Chaplain, mention my name, Buddy, mention my name."

We'd all been outside that store for several hours, knowing that there was death inside, and wanting it to end, no matter what it took. But at the last minute, the Suburban plan was scrapped: Stephens would have had too much time, after he spotted the truck roaring toward the store, to dispatch his wife and whoever else might remain inside.

The longer the day wore on, the more tense the situation became.

The resolution was both horrific and anticlimactic.

Stephens got drunk enough that his attention wandered momentarily, and his wife used the opportunity to dash from the store. A few minutes later, as I watched from my vantage point behind an ice cream truck, Stephens emerged, gun in hand.

Officers shouted: "DROP THE WEAPON!"

All the local TV stations were on the scene feeding live coverage to hundreds of thousands of viewers in the Dallas–Fort Worth area when Stephens raised the pistol and killed himself.

The police had been ready to kill this guy, if they had to. He'd tried to kill two people, and had succeeded in killing one. So, in some ways, it was easier to see him kill himself than it would have been for one of our guys to have done it. That would have compounded the whole situation. One of the officers would have been badly traumatized, and we'd be having to tell him that he'd only done what he had to do.

At least Stephens didn't put us through that.

And yet when that last shot rang out, I can't say that I was thinking anything like, "Good, it's finally over." Instead, I found myself thinking, what a complete waste. We were virtually begging him to put down the gun, and he was not doing it; he was hanging on to it. He didn't have to die.

So, when the shot rang out, I winced. I remember saying out loud: "No. Oh no. No!"

That night, on the way home, there was a woman on the interstate whose car had broken down. I stopped, showed her my badge and asked if I could help. She told me I could take her to some apartments where her friend lived.

She got in the car, and the first thing I found myself doing was telling her all about it. I don't usually talk about things like that, especially to total strangers. But I couldn't seem to stop. I remember thinking, "Well, this is really strange." Then I did the same thing to my wife when I got home. For about thirty minutes, I couldn't stop talking about it, just couldn't shut it off.

And then, all of a sudden, the floodgate came back down. All of a sudden, although I still wanted very badly to talk about it, I couldn't.

And then I couldn't sleep. I was serving as interim pastor at a Baptist church in the nearby town of Burleson, and I get intense about my sermons, and I remember thinking that getting into the pulpit the next morning would surely take my mind off the Stephens incident. But the next morning, in the pulpit, the mental tape just played, over and over again. It was crushed into my brain. It took another week before I could talk about it, and several more weeks before what I said about it made any sense.

On the one hand, those tapes are troublesome. You have to deal with them, sort them out. On the other hand, they do tend to make things very real, whether we want that or not.

At the time he pulled the trigger, the deranged man in front of the convenience store was just that: a deranged man in front of a convenience store, a total stranger, a stereotypical homicidal, suicidal maniac.

Over the next few days, however, bits and pieces of his story began to emerge, and it became clear that his life had become almost as tragic and senseless as his death. It's obvious that he needed help; what's tragic is that, though sporadically and maybe ineffectively, he had been trying by fits and starts to get it.

Stephens—a forty-year-old baggage handler for American Airlines—and his wife had separated several weeks before the deadly episode. Friends and co-workers told officers that he'd been abusive to his wife and children, and that the abuse had led Mrs. Stephens to file for divorce. But Stephens believed that her co-workers at the convenience store, Mrs. Palmer and Greg Talley, had egged her on toward the divorce.

Chronically abusive and domineering men have a need for power and control that is based in their own insecurity and is usually as a result of childhood emotional deprivation. When they feel threatened, they have a difficult time coping with their own emotions. Stephens ran true to type. Friends said that he had threatened his wife with that gun on other occasions, when she had so much as merely spoken to men—even customers.

His condition, while perhaps extreme, was far from insurmountable. Merely getting counseling helps between seventy and ninety percent of such men. They learn to express their feelings in appropriate ways, to relinquish some of their need for control, and to work toward relationships in which responsibilities are shared.

All this would be just so much pie in the sky, except for the fact that Stephens *had been* reaching out.

After his wife left him, Stephens, recognizing that his alcohol abuse was at least part of the problem, had checked into a group home run by the North Texas Alcohol and Drug Services, Inc. Staff there said he'd entered the home acutely depressed over his marital problems. He had been scheduled for release later in the month, but officials said that they had been planning to recommend that he stay another month at a minimum.

One of them told the press at the time: "When he was sober, he was the neatest person."

Human nature provides an unending source of irony.

As it was unfolding, live coverage of the story had the viewers glued to the set. It was, in short, a case where the television crews were providing exactly what the viewers' hunger for vicarious, no-risk excitement demands—why TV news exists in the first place.

This was no edited videotape; this was no talking-heads summation or interviews with sources close to events; this was the real thing. And viewers were dying to see how this all turned out. Would it be just semi-exciting, with the police saving the woman and arresting the man? Or would it be really exciting, with the police shooting the man?

And then, it ended, live, the way it did.

The man walked out of the store at about 6:30 p.m. Since it was the middle of January, it was dark, and lighting conditions in front of the store were not very good. About all that you could see on television was a silhouette in the corner of the screen that suddenly raised its hand to its head. You could hear the muffled bang, the noise diminished by the distortion of the microphones, and then you could see the silhouette falling down. It was in no way gory, because the picture was poor.

But at Channels 4, 5 and 8, the calls started coming in. "We didn't want to see this!" "Don't show us suicide! That's not drama, that's a bummer!" they said.

They called the newspapers, too, and the newspapers called the TV stations for a response to these "charges."

They got one from Jack Trammell, a producer at Channel 5. I think it was a good one, as it goes right to the point: "It was Einstein who said that reality is sometimes a tricky thing to manage."

It wasn't the fact that he had killed a convenience store clerk and then himself that caused the episode to keep receiving prominent play in the newspapers and broadcasts for the next several days. After all, double homicides and suicide/murders in the larger metro areas are news, but not big news—unless somebody famous is involved.

What kept it in the news was that it had been televised.

And these days, as we all know, it's not "real" unless it's on TV.

Remember those two wars? Both to fight communism,

both to prevent the Domino Theory, both in Asia? One we had protested, rightly or wrongly, and rightly or wrongly, one we didn't. What was the biggest difference between Korea and Vietnam? Nightly TV news made Vietnam a reality; we only read about Korea.

As the furor slowly receded into history, *Dallas Morning News* editorial-page chief Rena Pederson did some thoughtful musing in print. One friend of Mrs. Stephens, who recalled that Stephens had been behaving irresponsibly and threatening his wife, was quoted in the news as saying, "Aside from having him committed, there's not a soul in the world who could have prevented that from happening."

But maybe not. The Stephens family tragedy, which was brought into the living rooms of other families in a graphic way, points up the potential for violence in families. National estimates are that physical violence occurs in one out of four American families and that half of the children in those homes are battered as well.

And as the Stephens incidents showed, what used to be considered a "family matter" often escalates to the point where innocent people are killed.

Front-page stories like the Stephens case remind us how serious the problem of domestic violence is. Yet intervention efforts are still at a primitive, limited level. You can't help but wonder how things would have turned out if Thomas Edward Stephens could have been one of those helped.

Chapter 15

That some choose to end it all in the springtime of their lives, with all the joys and experiences still ahead of them, shocks us, depresses us—sometimes even stirs us to action. Funny, though, that we seldom get upset about a problem that is both larger and, in a way, sadder, than that of suicide among the elderly.

Older folk, facing those lean hardscrabble years in the late, dry autumn of life, take their own lives more than any other group. People over fifty, while making up roughly a quarter of the population, account for almost forty percent of all suicides. And there is reason to believe that, as more and more of the large "Baby Boomer" population crosses over into late life, those numbers will get higher.

That a larger population means greater numbers of suicides is no surprise; what is puzzling is that the RATES are also showing a dramatic increase: twenty-one percent over the past six years. A 1991 study co-authored by Richard Sattin of the Centers for Disease Control showed that in 1980, for every one million people older than sixty-five, 178 killed themselves. By 1986, the number had jumped to 215.

It is by and large a white-male problem. Almost three-quarters of the suicides among people over fifty are committed by men—and ninety-six percent of these men are white. Moreover, it was this group that was showing the greatest increase. The suicide rate for white men rose twenty-three percent from 1980 to 1986. (Sattin used 1980–86 figures because later figures were not complete.)

And suicide among this group are the least prevented and, to some extent, the least preventable.

Suicide among the elderly reflects some important differences between old and young. For one thing, those who attempt suicide usually succeed. Among the population as a whole, the ratio of attempted suicides is about ten to one—ten tries for each "success." In the young, it has been estimated to be as high as one hundred to one.

In the old, the ratio of successful to attempted suicide is one to one.

As the American Psychiatric Association's report on Mental Illness in Later Life put it: "When an old person attempts suicide he almost always fully intends to die."

The authorities put forward no guesses for the reasons for the increase—and in fact, express puzzlement. As late as 1980, it was generally predicted that the suicide rate in the elderly would go down. This was based on the theory that Social Security, Medicare, and advocacy groups for the elderly were making life easier for older people.

But financially and medically "easier" does not necessarily mean "better." And the belief that the problems of the elderly were being handled by the government and by advocacy groups may have caused some to individually neglect the emotional and familial needs of the elderly and thus increase their isolation. That trend is only exacerbated by the role of television as an isolating, individuating factor in our culture. The set is not only baby-sitting the kids, but it's influencing grandma, too. The steady barrage of youth-oriented advertising and programming can only make her feel more "out of it."

Also, suicide for the elderly has become almost fashionable, thanks to the increasing public debate over voluntary euthanasia. Some professionals examining the public response to suicide have often found no stronger response than cruel insensitivity. Many people feel that since older people have already led long lives, there is no need to be concerned. This attitude drives the elderly deeper into their loneliness and isolation, making it still harder for prevention programs to reach them. Feeling old, worthless and unworthy, they are the least likely to call a hotline or counselor for help.

These elderly suicides are, for the most part, not the manipulative attempts of someone trying to control someone else. These are serious suicides, borne of desperation, social desolation, and depression—sad circumstances under which a formerly productive life might end.

Another common denominator in many of the elderly suicides is that the victim did it because he "didn't want to be any trouble." In actuality, once they pull that trigger, they are quite literally nothing but trouble. Because the ripples that spread from the shattering event of a suicide may travel for generations.

Elizabeth Stone is an example of this. She is fighting back with all her might and main; her forthright attitude about seeking help in the wake of her father's suicide could, in fact, save her life. Her biggest regret is that she wasn't able to save his. She tried, and maybe it was an impossible task, since the old man was quite determined. But she will never know, and will always wonder—just one of the many negative legacies he's left her.

She is no longer as bitter about her father. She believes that his pain must have been so overwhelming that all other considerations became secondary to ending it. She does wish, though, that he had helped her help him. But the harder she tried, the harder he resisted.

Her father, Hiram Latham, was, by all accounts, one tough gentleman, a man of few words. In fact, it is a little hard for someone not familiar with Mr. Latham to figure out why his family would miss him, and for someone not familiar with suicide to understand why his personality would make psychological damage from his suicide even stickier.

"Once," Mrs. Stone recalls, "I was working as a nurse in a psychiatric facility, making rounds with the doctor. He'd interview a patient on admission, and sometime later he'd say to me, 'Do you know how that person would kill themselves if they were going to do it?' He could tell by their language. They'd use, in their normal conversation, violence-words."

The connections can sometimes even be morbidly amusing. For instance, a man who complains of having to "jump to their tune" or "jump when asked to do something" is also a fair candidate for jumping off a bridge.

Hiram Latham was always talking about "blasting" folks.

There is the conventional wisdom that the bigger they are the harder they fall, and, relative to suicide in the elderly, it's true. Part of the reason more men than women kill themselves in advanced years seems to be that men have a much more difficult time adjusting to the dependency that old age brings. The fall, for Latham as for many elderly suicides, began when his wife died of a stroke in 1989. She had served as a foil for many of his harder tendencies—and, in fact, had brought out the best in him.

"He'd always had Mother to nurture him, to balance and soften him all those years. He really did have a side of him that was deeply compassionate. He had just had it so hard growing up. But Mother was able to bring out the good part.

"He would support her in all her desires to be compassionate; she was sacrificial in helping people. He would take her to nursing homes to read to people and give them little gifts and things. They would rescue homeless people off the street. Once they found a family with three little children who were living in their car in a park, and they persuaded their church to help them get enough money for food and to get the family into a house. Things like that.

"But he had a personality change after she died. It was, I think, that he was angry that she had died before him. He'd always planned for the money he'd saved to support Mother for the rest of her life after he died. Daddy was always talking about death. I remember when I was nine, he said, 'I won't live 'til I'm forty; I'll die before then.' It was like someone was always throwing a wet blanket over my head.

"But he'd always thought he would die first because he worked so hard. He figured he'd be in an accident or have cancer or something, and had laid aside all that money so she could have an independent life after he died. He was very angry that she died first, and here he was, stuck with being all alone. And when she wasn't there, he just sort of fell apart. He was OK when he was with us, but it never seemed like he wanted to stay very long.

"I recognized the symptoms of depression right after Mother died. He couldn't sleep, and he talked about it all the time. And he didn't enjoy the things he had used to enjoy. I finally got him to go to a doctor; he wouldn't go to a psychiatrist, but he did go to the doctor. I made him promise that he would tell the doctor the things that were going on with him. After he heard them, the doctor put him on antidepressants right away."

The problem was, nobody ever saw him taking his medication, and he would change the subject if he was asked.

There was another big red flag.

Hiram Latham, at eighty-four, had an uncle, Edward Latham, who'd killed himself after his wife had died. And he had been eighty-four at the time. Hiram had been close to his uncle, and told Mrs. Stone that what Edward had done had been his way to end the misery.

Mrs. Stone had told him that that was not the right way, not what God wanted. They had all been strong in their faith, believing that if life gets hard, you just hang in there. And if you suffer, there's a reason.

But at some point Hiram just stopped believing that.

Mrs. Stone was trying to get him some help, but nobody else in the family seemed to think the situation was serious. Part of her problem was that her father was in Beaumont, and she was not. A brother in Beaumont had taken over the job of keeping an eye on the old man. She saw him only on infrequent visits.

About a year after his wife died, Hiram Latham started talking about wanting to end it all. And then he told Mrs. Stone that he had a plan. It was a very off-beat and gruesome one.

"He said that he knew how he was going to do it; he was going to electrocute himself. I said, 'Daddy! How terrible! How are you going to do that?'"

"Well," he said, "I have a hair dryer, and I'll just get in the bathtub and put it in the water and I'll just die immediately."

Mrs. Stone was shocked. "Oh, Daddy! Do you want to be found that way? Do you realize how you'd be found and all the things that go on? Do you really want to be seen that way, your last act on earth?"

And he said, "I don't care. I don't care. You don't know what this is like. You don't understand the suffering."

She had immediately told her brother about it. He, in turn, had told Latham's physician, who changed his antidepressant. But all it really accomplished was that Hiram felt he'd made a mistake telling his daughter about his plan, and he just stopped talking about it.

For a while.

Though he still had his own house, Latham was again living with Mrs. Stone's brother and his family in Beaumont. He'd tried it once before and it hadn't worked out. They had wanted him to stay, but he'd always felt as if he was in the way, that he didn't fit in. So he had returned to his own house for a few months. But that was even worse. The reminders of his dead wife summoned up her ghost, and he had plenty of time to brood. Then he broke his hip, and, since to him a nursing home was an unthinkable alternative, he was forced to move back in with his son.

The old man had always kept guns and had said strongly that he wouldn't hesitate to use them to protect his possessions and his family.

He had a gun while at his son's house.

And he started talking about how, "This gun is gonna end it. Gonna end it all. One of these days I'm just gonna go ahead and do it."

His son found the gun and took it out of the house, telling his father he would not have one while he was there. But the old man set about getting another one, and continued to talk the same way to his daughter-in-law.

Mrs. Stone kept telling them, "You've got to get him to a doctor. A doctor needs to know that he's that strong on doing it."

But they never did take him to a professional counselor.

"Given the fact he had always talked in violent terms, I think we heard it so much that we began to think, oh, that's just Dad. That's just his way."

And then Dad began the final phase: implementing the plan. He started making some major changes in his life, changes that Mrs. Stone feels should have tripped her alarms.

"He started talking about wanting to sell his house and put his money into CDs. Then he called my sister and me and said, 'If you don't get up here and get this stuff, I'm gonna give it away or sell it to someone else. You better get what you want out of that house, because I'm serious about selling it. I've listed it.'"

The siblings began the long process of getting the house in shape for sale. Meantime, Latham moved out of his son's house and into a retirement center. For a while there, his mood improved. He said he liked the center—an aging but elegant old hotel building. But soon it became apparent that he wasn't making any friends among the staff or other residents. Then he started complaining about the place.

During this period, he was sort of "dating." An old friend of his and his wife's started going out to eat together. She had a car and could drive, and he could not. Since she was doing the driving, he arrived at the conclusion that he was imposing on her. He would not ask her to take him anywhere he needed to go because of his pride, and he wouldn't think of paying for a cab.

He was, in fact, decreasing his mobility, increasing his isolation—and nurturing his reasons for killing himself.

As far as the family can tell, there was no particular trigger, and no abrupt change leading to the end. It just came, inevitably.

Chapter 16

Silence will not cure a disease. On the contrary, it will make it worse.—Leo Tolstoy

Elizabeth Stone is certain that depression runs in her family.

There was Edward, the uncle who killed himself.

Then there was her father.

And now there's her.

Unlike them, she has sought help for her depression—and has been seeing a therapist off and on over the years. So, when her father began to renew his promises to kill himself, she told her therapist. And the therapist, who is also an old friend, told her:

"Prepare yourself. Prepare yourself for the worst. Prepare yourself so that you won't feel responsible or guilty."

"I had been doing all that, or trying to. But way down deep inside, I kept telling myself: No. He won't really do that. He won't do that because he's always been so strong. He won't do that because of his religious beliefs. He won't do that because we've talked before about what it would do to us, the rest of the family. He won't do that..."

And then he did.

Mrs. Stone's young grandson was visiting from California. It was the first time he'd been old enough to stay away from his parents with other relatives, so it was a special occasion.

It was the Monday morning after Father's Day. Mrs. Stone had tried to call her father that morning, but the line was busy. She waited an hour or two, and was about to call him again, when the phone rang.

Her brother said, "Elizabeth..." and she could tell by the tone of his voice what would follow: "It's happened."

"No—DAD?"

"Yeah."

Funny thing is, she didn't even have to ask if he'd died a natural death, like anyone else. She knew.

"How did he do it?"

"With a gun."

A strange feeling takes hold at a time like that. I've felt it myself—but I am sad to say that more often, in my job as bearer of very bad tidings, I have produced it in many, many others. It's a feeling that you've just been kicked in the stomach, hard... but it's coupled with a kind of amazement that you're still standing, and that it doesn't really hurt yet. So your eyes go kind of flat and wide and you start attending to little details, getting information, because you know that when the pain does set in, it's going to be incapacitating.

So she said, "Eddie, tell me just a little bit. Not too much, I'm not ready yet. Did he do it in his room?"

"No. Down the hall, there was kind of a little utility room by the elevator. He went in there. He put the gun in his mouth..."

"No! That's enough! No more."

And there began Mrs. Stone's journey into the twilight realm of an altogether different kind of shock and grief.

When her mother had died two years earlier, Mrs. Stone recalled, "I had the deepest grief I'd ever had in my life—but I didn't mind people comforting me. If they wanted to come and hug me, they could. I would cry when they did, but I could talk about it. Of course, I still felt deep, horrible sadness for almost a year. I'd cry when I'd hear a song that was one of her favorites. When I saw someone who knew her, I would get real emotional. But it was sooo different with Daddy..."

First, a big withdrawal. "I didn't want anyone to know about it. We couldn't do anything immediately anyway. My grandson—Bobby, who is eight—had a ticket to fly back to California two days later, and his parents wouldn't be there to receive him until then, so we had to keep him. I wanted to keep him. We focused on him. It was our first time to have a grandchild come and stay with us, so it was a real special time.

"I didn't want any of my friends coming, and I didn't want anyone to talk about it around Bobby and upset him. We just told him that Grandpa had died, and that we were real sad, but we wanted to go ahead and enjoy his visit. I was careful not to tell him how Grandpa died; I just told him that Grandpa was real, real old, in his middle eighties. And he didn't ask any questions. He was sad.

"So I was pushing everything off at arm's length. I think I was trying to protect myself as much as anyone else, rather than face the pain, the reality of it. But as soon as we got Bobby on the plane on Wednesday we took off for Beaumont. We got there just a few hours before the funeral."

And of course the funeral directors had begun to work their revisionist magic. "I was surprised when the funeral director recommended that we have an open casket. He said they had been able to repair enough of Daddy's face that it wasn't so bad, just a little swollen. He thought it would help everybody to accept this, rather than wonder what he looked like and let their imagination take them to the pits imagining all these horrible scenes (which had, of course, actually occurred). The funeral director said he felt it was best for the last time to see him looking sort of like himself, and not destroyed."

An argument can be made that we should protect the family from that reality, particularly in cases of suicide. But I can make an equal case for the point that having the opportunity to at least imagine Grandpa as he might be "naturally" under that closed coffin lid, is helpful, particularly in cases of suicide.

Because in the family of a suicide, the biggest legacy is often more suicide. Some suicidologists estimate that suicide among survivors is between eighty and three hundred percent higher than the general population.

Those who are left are actually suffering under a triple assault—from the death itself, from the rejection by the one who left, and from the disillusionment felt for his having done so. These three factors produce a loss of self-worth in the mourner, and an anger for which he may see only himself as an appropriate target.

Still other factors come crowding in. Did the suicide in effect "give permission" to the rest of the family to take this hardest of easy ways out? Does one of the survivors unrealistically idolize the deceased to the extent that he sees his actions as being unquestionably right—and will he thus copy the means of his demise?

Mrs. Stone is staring that one square in the face in the case of a younger brother. "He has said that he thought Daddy's suicide was a very courageous and altruistic act, that rather than spend all his money on nursing homes and bills, he ended it and still left a little money to all of his children. I tried to argue with him, telling him that he doesn't know that much about suicide. People mostly do it just for themselves."

Then there's the simple fact that a suicide manages to produce grief, guilt, and anger in the survivor. This is the recipe for depression—and depression is the chief ingredient in suicide. The suicide also produces the disease in the survivor—and simultaneously withdraws the cure, which is communication.

In more mundane death situations, the surviving family takes a healthy first step toward dealing with their psychological and emotional damage just by talking to each other about it. It's God's way of helping us to get used to this inevitable loss. We need to express our feelings. Mourning can never be complete until we've had a chance to talk about how we feel about the person who died, and to talk about our pain and anger over his departure.

Yet this avenue is frequently closed to the survivors of suicide, because the family does not want to expose the shame, blame, and guilt they feel, as Elizabeth Stone learned. The central fact that the death was suicide colors all other considerations. After her father's suicide, this manifested itself as a complete inability to accept comfort. "I was very suspicious of everybody. I didn't want anybody to bring any food over to the house after the funeral because I didn't want to talk to anybody. I didn't want any questions. I told only one person that he'd killed himself, and I let other family members handle the rest."

That one person had had a suicide in her own family, and suggested that Mrs. Stone talk to her about Hiram's suicide. Mrs. Stone thanked her, but told her she had talked to family and ministers. The friend wouldn't let it drop, and Mrs. Stone became very angry.

"I'll talk to whom I want to, when I want to. Now get off my back!"

For the quiet, grandmotherly, and deeply religious Mrs. Stone, this was a major explosion. But there were others to come. The fact that the triple burden of blame, shame, and guilt make communication difficult is often compounded by helpful people who make things worse— like the following interchange with one of her consolers:

"Elizabeth, I'm here for you, and I want you to know that everybody wants you to come and let us give you a hug and support you any way we can."

"I appreciate it. But I'm just really not ready for that yet."

"And we were just wondering, uh, was he sick?"

"Well, no, he was aging, and he just died."

"Well, we were just wondering—how did he die?"

"Well, he took his own life."

"Did he? Oh, he didn't! Well, we thought he did!"

"That made me furious. It made my toes curl. Because it confirmed that it was a topic of gossip among all my friends, and fodder for speculation. It was just so disrespectful."

And she pauses a moment, and then blurts it out:

"Flat ashamed! That's the word I'm dancing around here. Flat ashamed! I was ashamed. I was deeply disappointed in my father."

Chapter 17

A hard rock hits the yielding water, making a big splash. Big waves extend in all directions, becoming smaller, becoming wavelets, then ripples, then riplets, and then perhaps just a barely visible shimmer: A minuscule rise, an almost imperceptible fall.

But though these motions become too small to be easily seen, still they exist, still they manifest themselves, still they affect circumstances farther down the line. And so still waters really aren't, not ever; still waters really do run deep.

It's like echoes of thunder or gunfire. They fade away— but below the level of human hearing, at a level beneath our grasping but no less real and perhaps only heard by dogs or angels or eternity, there are repercussions, reverberations. And sometimes, repetitions.

Echoes and ripples: What happened back then shapes what happens right now; and what happens right now, shapes what happens later on.

That self-evident truth scares Ben Johnson. Because many, many years ago his soft young life was hit by a big hard rock.

Ben Johnson was four and playing innocently in his yard when his mother went in the house, locked the bathroom door, and shot herself.

That was in 1956. Eisenhower was president.

Ben and his big brother were out playing in the yard, and didn't hear the blast. But then their daddy came home and asked where their mother was. They didn't know, but started looking for her. Their daddy got the bathroom door unlocked, but there was still something obstructing it. It seemed that maybe their mom had fallen in front of the door. But then their daddy went outside and around to the window. Then he screamed, "Oh My God..."

Ben Johnson is forty-one now.

He's still riding the crest of that wave that spread from his knowledge of his mother's suicide, a wave almost two decades old, still wondering where it will peter out, still wondering how it will end. Wondering, worse still, if it will ever end.

Ben Johnson also knows something he wishes he didn't know—that suicide is always an option, that a shotgun to the side of his head can get him out of just about anything.

And he knows that one wave engenders another.

It is the nature of the Universe. For every cause, there's an effect; for every action, a result. And the darkest knowledge of all—and the only solid lesson left him by his mother—is that everything that begins must have an ending, and humans can choose where and how and when it ends.

And he has a couple of questions for which he will never know the answer: Is he still a child now? Or was he ever fully a child?

Ben Johnson has children of his own. Sometimes that really blows him away.

He wonders, in the dark of the darker nights, if it might someday blow them away too. On what distant shore will this wave finally break, this echo fade away?

There are really two Ben Johnsons. One is Gentle Ben, a man remarkable for the depth of his devotion to his wife and children and to his friends. Ben Johnson wants to be seen as a solid, normal member of the human race, and he works at it. He is an easy person to be with because he's had to work at it.

But there is also another Ben Johnson—Dark Ben, a man with a big, gray cloud hanging over his shoulder. That cloud has shaded his whole life with somber hues, coloring it in ways he's still grappling to understand.

In the past several years he has found what a

psychologist might term "an appropriate outlet" for the darkness. He pours it out through his pen and his guitar in the songs he writes and sings. Even the lighter, happier of these tunes reveal a backdrop of mourning and sadness. It is clear that Ben has learned to grab and savor the joyful times when they come along.

The darker of Johnson's musical efforts raise chill bumps.

Ben says that it's a strange and nebulous kind of darkness that he lives with inside his head, because it contains no answers, only unanswerable questions. The darkness is more an absence than a presence. The funny thing is, Ben Johnson cannot tell you what it is like for your mother to commit suicide. Since he was only four years old at the time, he has nothing else to compare his life to.

He can only acknowledge those ripples and echoes, and try to make sense of his confusion.

Adding to Johnson's sprawling gray confusion is that, for years, no one told him his mother had killed herself. He was sixteen, in fact, before his brother Bud, Ben's senior by eleven years, let slip the fateful fact.

"My brother was talking about her and said, 'Yeah, before she killed herself, she...' and it was the first time anyone had ever spoken the words. I must have known it, because it didn't just floor me. It was like, hmmm, yeah. So somewhere in the back of my mind I must have known it, but that was the first time anyone had flat said it, used the words, killed herself."

In retrospect, Johnson sees that his whole family was in some kind of denial.

"They just didn't talk about it. Mother was this distant image on a pedestal, always, 'your mother, bless her heart' and 'poor Mom, poor Mom, she was an angel.' That sort of stuff. It was kind of a dark subject. We'd built up this myth around her to keep from talking about her."

Ben had tried the direct approach a time or two, like once when he was ten. He asked his father, point-blank, "How did Mother die?"

Bailey Johnson's reply was, "We'll talk about it when you're older."

Ben's family—and particularly his father, who must have been dealing with a great deal of his own guilt—indulged Ben's every whim. The word No was seldom used. Ben remembers visits to his Dallas cousins, the family of J. W. and Eula Mae Sanderson, when he would play with his second cousin and lifelong friend, Bill.

"I remember being over there and Bill would say, 'Mama, can we have a Coke?' and Mrs. Sanderson would say, 'No, you've already had a Coke today.'

"And I'm like: What!!! You can't have a Coke??? Unreal! It must be pretty rough over at your house. No Coke!"

Looking back through his childhood, Johnson cannot recall anyone telling him to do anything, ever. "I don't remember having any kind of schedule or structure or anything. I would eat what I wanted to, when I wanted to. I was pretty spoiled, loose, indulged."

But these indulgences, coupled with the somewhat sacrosanct mystery surrounding the memory of his mom, only further served to set him apart.

"As my dad used to put it, I just didn't take to spoiling. I think part of this Mom Deal is that I felt almost inferior, real cowed. I was withdrawn, quiet—and really holding back a lot of stuff."

That sense of apartness has stayed with him to some degree all his life. What is it he fears is missing from himself?

"That's the problem. How would I know? What's missing is an answer to that question. For example, me and a guy were talking one time, just shooting the breeze, and he said something about, 'Yeah, you know, how a Mother gives you that special feeling...' And I just sat there like a dog cocking his ears at a strange noise, like, 'No, I don't. You got me, Buddy. How is it?'"

Each of us lacks something, and we cannot know what it would be like to have that thing, or what our lives would be like if we had it. But a mother is a pretty central thing to have never had—and that absence, which has colored every aspect of Ben Johnson's life, has also made almost every decision and impulse fraught with the ambiguity of the unknowable.

There is little doubt in Johnson's mind, though, that the closer he got to that which he feared the most—marriage and domestic life—the more he drank. During this time there were several violent episodes, and after each of these, Ben Johnson thought of suicide. "I thought about it a lot more than I'd like to admit, particularly in the aftermath of these violent episodes. I'd wake up feeling guilty and embarrassed and stupid and pointless and I'd think: I'll just get out of here. I'll just check out. The thing here is, for better or worse, my mother was still a role model: Face it, here's what Mom did. It opens that option."

What stopped him?

"I guess I had more sense than I thought I did. One side said, 'Let's just get out of here.' But the other side said, 'Well, look what she did when SHE did it.' It didn't help anything, and it hurt a lot of people."

It was also in Johnson's early twenties that he found himself standing in a field cold sober but still out of his mind. It was almost as if his instinct for self-preservation had finally brought him to take the first steps toward what was needed.

"I was just standing there screaming and crying, bellowing up to the sky—to my mom—I didn't know what to take it all out on, so I just stood out there screaming obscenities at her, and asking her why? As it turns out, that was a real good and healthy thing to do, very cathartic. It was just too bad I didn't do it when I was four instead of twenty-two. The big question I had for her was WHY? Why couldn't you have lasted another day? Why couldn't she find some solution other than that? Because the thing about suicide is, you don't really know what you are doing to everyone else. Or, worse, there's the flip side: What if you DO know what you're doing to everyone else, and you do it anyway? That's such a negation, such an insult. If you do know all the ripples you're going to cause, all the misery, it's almost like you deserve to be dead."

Lois Johnson had attempted suicide earlier, drinking carbolic acid when she was about twenty and had thought that Bailey was not going to marry her. She'd succeeded in giving herself stomach trouble that would plague her through the years.

Bailey and Lois Johnson were in many respects a classic example of a couple in which suicide is statistically more likely to occur—the two were diametric opposites, and Lois was the more self-effacing and withdrawn of the pair.

In recalling Lois Johnson, the words "aloof" and "reserved" pop up frequently. Bailey Johnson, on the other hand, was a go-getter, a wheeler-dealer. He was out to conquer the world. He'd make big deals to buy land and build houses and then, rather than nest-egging the proceeds, he'd pour it all back into the next big deal. And he'd buy things, like the sprawling ranch-style house sitting on a lake and twenty acres of land just outside Dallas. Then he'd refinance the house and take off after another deal. And for a while there, it had worked out fine.

"His feeling was always that if you can't go first-class, don't go—and he went," says Ben. "That attitude made him a lot of money, at first. And then a couple of those deals didn't work; rather than gamble half of what he had, he gambled everything, and lost."

Lois Johnson handled the books and juggled the family finances and robbed Peter to pay Paul: She knew just how much trouble they were in.

Bailey, by nature of his personality and sometimes overweening self-confidence, had gotten in way deeper than he could dig himself out, and Lois told a friend she was going to leave.

The banks and creditors started closing in. And then the IRS moved in for its pound of flesh. Coupled with her depression, it was the last straw. Lois killed herself on April 15, 1956, right at tax time.

She'd left the Bible open to a verse: "Give unto the Lord the glory due unto his name: bring an offering, and come before him: worship the Lord in the beauty of holiness."

Exactly what those lines meant to her no one knew—but for at least two or three years after her death, about all Bailey Johnson could do was sit in his big house, reading that verse, and crying, while his world continued to fall in on his head.

Ben doesn't remember much about his mother before she died—a flash here, a snapshot there. He remembers images of her and his father dancing together. He remembers that on the day she died all these people came over to the house, and he remembers wondering why there was such a big party if things were bad.

He remembers people telling him over and over that everything would be OK, when he really wasn't sure what was wrong. He remembers the huge vault in the ceiling at Pleasant Mound Methodist Church. He remembers the huge mound of flowers. And for a long time, before he identified this memory, he could not go into a florist's shop without getting the willies.

Then there was that long period during which he remembers his father being sad. It may be then that Ben Johnson began to compartmentalize his young life. He had been a happy-go-lucky, fun-loving child, others say, which is distinctly at odds with the withdrawn, self-absorbed boy Ben Johnson remembers being. Part of that facade may have been mimicry; since he didn't know how he was supposed to feel, he tried to learn how to act.

Sometimes Bailey would take Ben and his cousins to what the kids called "The Garden." The Garden was in fact Grove Memorial Park, where Lois Johnson was buried.

I've been there many times. It's a sad, beautiful, evocative place. I can almost see Bailey Johnson out there sitting on a tombstone by his dead wife's grave. And I can almost feel the contrast between his thoughts and those of the children, playing nearby. It's a very quiet place to spend a peaceful moment taking a break from the middle of your own story—to see how it will end.

Time gets lost out here, and thus, in a way, so does Life.

And over by the statue of a weeping angel, people like Bailey Johnson can sit and ponder, as cicadas sizzle in the trees, and mourning doves lament another summer away. In this garden, then, the strange contrasts between life and death, between a son playing in the grass and a dead wife's grave, between butterflies and last year's leaves, raise questions.

And then the remaining Johnsons, saddled with debt, were forced to move to a smaller place, to leave the sprawling spread of expensive, close-to-town land that Bailey Johnson had acquired.

Whether because of the times or its association with a suicide, the big long and rambling Johnson house, now dark-windowed and lonesome on its big grounds, remained empty, slowly slipping into neglect and disrepair, haunted by the knowledge that a suicide had taken place in it.

And most of the kids from the area around Samuel Adams School went there, at one time another, for one reason or another.

Among them was Tommy H., who later got very seriously into drugs as a young adult, and blew his brains out on Christmas morning.

Suicide.

Sharon E., also from the general neighborhood, later drank a combination of rubbing alcohol and followed it with a large quantity of barbiturates.

Greg S., who hanged himself.

Su-i-cide.

Echo? Ripple? Coincidence?

Ripples and echoes, dying, diminishing with the passage of time—but Johnson wonders if they will ever be gone.

Johnson's most devout hope is that the violent storm that broke on his lineage in 1956 will end with him, or at least become vastly diminished—and that the means of his own end will serve as a good model.

Chapter 18

Sometimes death is so much like a drunk driver it's little wonder they sometimes go hand in hand.

Death is out of control, oblivious to human consequences, all over the road with no clear aim. Death, like a drunk, seems to confuse horsepower with omnipotence, willfulness with willpower. Death is unswayed by logic or love or decency, and is determined only that nothing will deter him from pursuit of his perverse pleasures.

Death doesn't think. Death just gets behind the wheel and goes—and so death comes crashing into lives like a cold dark obscene wave.

And Death was drunk when he came swooping out of the late-night darkness of October 9, 1992, doing nearly seventy mph in a forty-five mph zone, sitting behind the wheel of a flatbed truck.

When someone called the station to report the truck, Officer Terry Lynn Lewis, thirty-five, and reservist Jerry Crocker, forty-three, were busy doing the Samaritan thing for which they had something of a reputation within the police department.

Only a few days before, Terry Lewis had worked a case of Indecency With a Child: a sixteen-year-old boy had forced his way into a low-income apartment and fondled a fourteen-year-old girl. Per department policy, Terry Lewis' supervisor had told him to let the juvenile division handle it. But the mother of the girl had expressed concerns about leaving the girl alone in the apartment the next day; she had to work until 8:00 p.m., and was scared the boy would come back while she was gone.

The next day had been Lewis' day off. He nevertheless went and picked the girl up at school and took her back to the apartment, where he made arrangements for someone to keep her until her mother got off work.

And on this October evening, he and his reservist partner had just dropped off a woman whose car had been damaged by a hit-and-run driver.

Lewis had been an "above and beyond the call of duty" kind of officer since his first day on the force, nine months before—and even before that.

I'd known him longer than anyone at APD, I guess. He and my oldest daughter, Sherrie, had gone to school together. And I'd married him to his wife, Kris, way back in 1977. Like so many Arlington young people, they'd both worked at Six Flags. He'd told Kris once, only half-joking, that he'd lived the perfect life: "I've been a cowboy, a firefighter and a policeman. What else could a boy want?"

He had in fact managed a ranch and been a volunteer fireman before returning to Arlington in 1983 to go to work for his family's office-supply house. One of Lewis' clients was the city of Arlington, and business brought Lewis frequently to the station house.

He was one of those guys who just sort of slipped in to our police department. He used to service our typewriters and other machines, and started hanging out more and more. It just sort of grew on him, and he grew on us. Soon, he'd taken a job as a jailer, waiting for a slot to come open at the police academy. Next thing, he was going through the academy. Next thing, he was a full-fledged rookie police officer.

The next thing, both he and his partner were dead.

Something at the funeral brought this back to me; it's kind of a funny way to remember a guy, but it's pure Terry Lewis.

He begged me all the time to be the speaker at his Optimist Club luncheons. And a lot of times, I would do it—even though I knew better. Because each time I was there, every time I would stand up to make my talk, no matter what the subject—serious, sad, funny, informative, it didn't matter—he'd wait until I got going, and then he'd find some excuse to pop out some comment, just to interrupt me.

This happened several times, and I finally said, "Terry, don't do that. Just don't do that anymore. You invited me here, now, at least be polite enough to let me speak."

And he would apologize and promise it wouldn't happen again. And sure enough I'd go back to the Optimists, and sure enough, he'd stand up and do it again.

For his funeral, more than three thousand people were there—including law enforcement officers, people from his church, and his softball and Little League teams. By official estimate there were fifteen hundred civilians and another fifteen hundred officers on hand, many lined up in an honor guard outside the church, along with dozens of members of the media.

Assisting me in the service was the pastor of his Methodist Church. He hadn't been around long enough to get to know all the members of the Lewis family intimately.

One of Terry's daughters is named Nina. So is his mother. But the difference is that his daughter pronounces her name "Neenah," while the mother pronounces hers "Nynah," and the pastor made the mistake of referring to the daughter as "Nynah."

And so what does she do? She stands right up in the middle of the service and says, "It's not NYNAH, it's NEENAH!"

So much like father like daughter that I didn't know whether to laugh or cry, so I did a little of both.

Terry Lewis left three very tough little daughters—Becky, fourteen, Ann, twelve, and Nina, nine.

Nobody knew how tough until a few days later. They'd had their hysterical moments, those tear-drowned, grief-choked moments when they gave in to the feeling that their entire world had come unglued and fallen in on them. But each time they fell into the depths of utter despair, they'd managed to scrabble back out of the pit—

and were staying out, after about a week, for longer periods of time with each passing day.

They were staying out long enough, in fact, that the shock could be held at bay long enough to ask themselves some questions, like why couldn't the paramedics save their father and Jerry Crocker? They save people all the time, don't they?

They were told it was a bad wreck.

How bad? they asked. Unsurvivable, they were told.

That was not good enough. They insisted on seeing the car.

And several officers accompanied them to the city auto pound.

Away from public view and covered by a tarp to discourage gawking eyes was what was left of the squad car.

I've seen hundreds of wrecks, many of them fatalities, but it was a physical shock for me the first time they lifted that tarp.

After they had dropped off the hit-and-run victim at the Remington Meadows Apartments, Lewis and Crocker had pulled out and probably never saw what hit them. Skid marks indicated that after the flatbed hit them broadside on the front and rear doors, it pushed their car another 105 feet. The reinforced bumper of the flatbed crushed the left exterior of the car all the way through the interior until it was almost flush with the right passenger door, and bent the frame into a U.

Only a miracle could have saved them, and there wasn't one that night.

While the three girls surveyed the awesome wreckage, officers all around the car had tears in their eyes. Some were weeping quietly but openly, both for their dead friends and for the three girls and Kris as they stood there trying to make sense of what had happened during their father's last few seconds on earth.

But the girls are not crying. And after they've looked a long, long time, one of them turned to the policemen and said, "OK. Now we understand."

One officer, in a tribute to their resilience, summed

the scene up like this: "Girls, 1; Cops, 0."

Other than the fact that policemen were involved, the deaths of Terry Lewis and Jerry Crocker were your average random, violent, untimely deaths—if, of course, there is such a thing as random, violent, untimely, and "average."

There was no big high-speed chase, no gripping, dramatic shootout. It could have as easily been two nice, mostly average salesmen pulling out of that parking lot heading home after a late sales pitch as two nice, mostly average cops getting ready to go off duty in thirty minutes.

But since they were officers, after their deaths that status got them some things other people don't get, like honor guards, and other policemen coming in from all over Texas and the Southwest to represent their various departments. Their families got police escorts everywhere they went, and round the clock security at home for the first couple of weeks after the tragedy.

All of which is entirely appropriate, as these people, more than any other kind of public servant except perhaps for soldiers at war, willingly lay their lives on the line every day. In addition to all the other things, they got media attention. Print reporters typed reams. TV and radio folks recorded reel after reel. The news "hook" was "Cops Killed by Drunk Driver."

But somehow the story managed to shake off the news hook and the "specialness" and the apartness of police officers and present itself for what it really was—a tale of Average Death, and just how hellish death is.

In every breathless news report one could read between the lines and know: This happens all the time, and goes unremarked, unnoticed, and certainly unresearched and unexpanded; most of the time it's a one-column headline over a two-paragraph story on an inside page—if it's mentioned at all.

Police officers know this better than anyone.

It did not hit me until much later that whether it's an accident, homicide and suicide, the internal reactions are the same. Grief, rage, even a little guilt. It is the expression of these that varies.

In a homicide, you may vent rage at the killer.

In an accident, you may rail against the cause of the accident, or the person or agency whose negligence caused it.

In suicide, the dead one and the loved one are the same. But the rage is there.

There are some convergences of time, place, and circumstance that become, for an hour or two, absolutely sacred, with or without benefit of clergy. Such a moment occurred in the home which Terry Lewis had left to his wife, Kris, and those three daughters.

The family had asked me to be there for an interview, in case it became something undesirable. But it turned out that I was not needed. In fact, I felt blessed to be there.

Because this was good journalism. It had a purpose, one that what was left of Terry Lewis' family could get foursquare behind. The TV station, Channel 8, just happened to be doing a serious feature series on drunk driving at the time of the Lewis and Crocker fatalities. And the station had been gracious enough to wait a week after the funeral to pursue the Lewis angle.

And then they had sent a reporter with sense and grace enough to know that it was a privilege and not a right for her to be there, and that the mother, wife, and daughters of Lewis were willing to allow some gentle probing of their suffering if it would save one single life and prevent one family from having to go through their shattered misery.

Sometimes the camera can look straight into the human soul.

Sitting clustered together on a beige couch in the living room of the neat, middle-class Lewis home, three daughters, a wife, and a mother looked straight into the camera lens and poured through it their abysmal grief and subdued anger—not just at the drunk driver in the Tarrant County Jail who had broken up their happy home, but also at Death lurking out there in the darkness beyond.

They talked down, way down, to the drunk. But they stood up to Death.

When the interview began, Kris Lewis looked as small

and forlorn and bereft as she felt.

The interviewer said, "Let's just get this rolling by asking, how are you feeling right now, about the... "

Kris said, "Numb, lost," so inaudibly that the interviewer asked that the central air be turned off so the mikes could pick up her voice.

"Tell me about your children," the reporter urged.

"They're very angry. That man (the drunk driver) should be in that box instead of their dad. Or he should have been standing right there at the funeral, watching what they were doing at that point in time."

And what kind of effect has this had on your family?

"It's turned our lives upside down. We're trying to stay focused, but we were close. We're still close, but we're confused, and we're trying... we ARE going to go on. We're not quitters. So we'll go on. But our lives have been completely changed at this point. We are simply going to have to get used to it."

What would she say to the flatbed driver at this point?

"Honestly, at this point, I don't have anything to say. At this point, all I could do is stare at him and cry. Because what happened to Terry shouldn't have happened. It could have been prevented, but it happened. And right now, I don't have any words. I'm numb. I think it'll come, but right now I'm numb."

Nina (Neenah) interrupted: "My dad isn't going to be here when I graduate from high school or college, or when I have kids. I would ask the driver, WHY? Why did he get behind the wheel? He might not have even been able to stand up. Why would he try to drive? Who will help me with my homework? My dad was always here, helping me out... "

What do they hope comes out of all this?

Kris said: "That this will stop. Something good has to come of it; that's the only way I can deal with it. Let me just say something here: If something good comes out of this, well, it won't be worth it, but if it helps somehow, if it makes a difference, we can handle it. If someone else can be saved, we all would want that."

Nina: "Dad included."

Kris Lewis, a competent airline employee, had been at work at DFW (Dallas–Fort Worth Airport) when a supervisor stuck her head in the door, asked the other girls to leave the room, and said, "Somebody's here to see you, Kris."

And Kris Lewis had said, "OK."

She can still clearly see the policemen, her husband's friends, walking through the door, and she recalls thinking, "My gosh, what are THEY doing here?" And then her own father came through the door and she smiled and said, "Dad, wow, are we having a party? What's the deal?"

There was a long silence, and that's when it hit her.

"If you've never experienced it, it's a lot different from being prepared for someone dying. It was shock. I was very numb, very upset. We sat for a while and didn't say anything. Then I started picking up my stuff and realized that my wedding ring, which I'd broken a week earlier, was still at the jeweler's being fixed. And I told my dad, 'If only I'd had my ring...'"

From her office, they all just went straight to the Lewis home. Other than the fact that it was very quiet, her memories are vague, as though she were seeing her life through a scrim.

"I guess Sgt. Bill Stallsworth told me about the accident, but that's still all kind of hard to remember... it's all a blur. I'm still just going through the motions until the pieces start coming back together and we can figure out what to do from here."

The Channel 8 interviewer asked about her finances.

"Terry is still taking care of me right now, that's all I can say at this point. Our lives have just been completely changed, snapped. In the blink of an eye. Completely. A blink. That's all I can stress: A simple blink of an eye. Everything has changed."

The interviewer, sensing that maybe she was starting to impose, said, "I'll conclude with this one last question."

But it was a good one, leading to another half-hour of remembrance, grief, and anger. Kris Lewis is one of life's quiet tigers. She's friendly but shy and somewhat reticent—but show her the proper prey—like the reporter's question—and look out.

"What would you tell anyone right now who might be thinking about getting behind the wheel of a car after drinking?"

And the self-effacing reticence—even some of the shock of loss—disappeared. Kris Lewis leaned forward and spoke very distinctly: "Don't!

"THIS is what's left behind. We're talking friends, not only adult friends; we are talking about my children's friends, my children's teams—softball, football. We're talking about an entire police department. It goes on. It's bigger than a family tree.

"Don't do it. One afternoon has so completely changed people's lives. Totally."

The interviewer felt she was getting to the meat of the matter, and asked how the drunk driver should be punished?

"Make him talk to the family," spat Nina, outraged, glowering at the camera through tears and snuffles.

Kris paused a moment, at first to smooth her daughter's emotions, almost as if to shush her and say, That's not nice.

And then she reconsidered. She agreed. "Yes—set up a two-way mirror," said Kris, firm and clear. "Let him see us as we are. Let him be here and let him feel all of it. Nobody can possibly comprehend it unless they've experienced it personally. They can't comprehend the feelings, they can't comprehend the scenes, a husband and father in a box. Make him get right up close. Make him be there for the initial shock. Make him be there when the kids hear the news. Let him walk unseen into that room when Harold and I first had to tell them, or let him stand outside that window and hear what happens when you have to wake them up and say, 'Your father's dead. Here's what happened.'"

Right after I left the Lewis home that day, I was called out to a suicide. This one was unusual because one of the family members, the ex-wife, went off on a very strong verbal expression of rage at the deceased. She was angry—angry at the misery that the suicide had added to a family already under stress.

The victim had been very dependent on the rest of the family, emotionally. They had been trying to provide the help and support they felt he needed, but were failing at it. He had a graduate degree and had in the past had some high-paying jobs, but for a variety of reasons, one of which was alcohol, he could not hold a job.

Their troubles had led the couple to split, but even afterwards the family had tried to be there for him as best they could. When his body was found in his apartment, there were two letters of rejection from companies he'd applied to.

He had an insurance policy, worth about two hundred thousand, and it was an insurance policy that would pay in the event of suicide. He had apparently figured he was worth more to them dead than alive. So he'd thought about everything very carefully—everything except the misery that he was going to heap on his already guilt-ridden family.

His wife had an additional burden. Her mother had also committed suicide years earlier.

She was very angry. She said, "What Mother did to me, now he's doing to my daughters."

She had been roughly the same age as her daughters when her mother had killed herself.

It could be said that Terry Lewis left his family emotionally in the best condition they could ask for under the circumstances. Which is true. And it could be said of the other guy, given the divorce and his unemployment, that he left them in the worst, other than financially.

There are happier endings than Terry's and Kris'—but no ending is truly happy. Because endings aren't happy. It's beginnings and middles that are fun. The best you can ask of an ending is that it doesn't spoil all that came before.

Chapter 19

My job takes me daily to the "local" darknesses, into those dark patches of life obscured by sudden squalls of pain and cold sheets of hurt and death, to most of the murder, suicide, and accidental-death scenes of this average suburb. I can't make the dark clouds go away, but I can hold up an emotional umbrella and try to point the survivors to shelters of support.

My vocation compels me to move quickly into these sudden local darknesses and do what I can. But preservation of my peace of mind and perhaps even my sanity compels me to move just as quickly back out into life and the sun as soon as my job is done.

Twenty-four hours a day, American Christian Television Service (ACTS) goes out coast-to-coast, and the hopeless, helpless callers come. COPE, one of the network's invaluable shows, airs five hours a week. For some of those hours, Harold Elliott answers calls.

What can I tell a total stranger who's also a potential suicide in the course of a few minutes as I stare blindly out at him in his too-dark living room from his too-bright TV set, dealing with what may be the biggest crisis of his life?

The bottom line, all I can really tell him is, "Help is available, and we can start right here."

People are dying to talk about suicide, and each time I come back on the air and people line up seeking help to keep them from self-destructing.

The studio is big, darkened, and cavernous, usually empty and still and echo-y except for the bright little set and the small island of technicians silently watching their dials.

As in most talk-show formats, the host, Dr. Karen Hayter, introduces me and we exchange pleasant chit-chat for a few moments.

"Harold, over the years that you've been recognized as an authority on suicide, I guess one of the most often-asked questions is, 'Is suicide a sin?'"

"The question, Karen, is, can you go to heaven if you kill yourself? Is it a sin? I believe, yes. You're destroying something God created for God's own reasons. *You* didn't give yourself life, and so you shouldn't take it away. But the other half is, no, I don't believe that it's an *unpardonable* sin. We are not judged by how we die, but by how we live and to whom we have committed our lives. Survivors of suicide say, 'Well, I've been taught that it was an unpardonable sin,' or, 'Our church believes so and so.' But in my opinion it's not so much a doctrine as a traditional belief, a belief that has come down through the centuries."

In the earliest Christian church, many Christians went willingly into the lions' den to gain martyrdom. St. Augustine sought to stop that by circulating the notion that it was unpardonable. Thus they were able to stop the overzealous from volunteering for martyrdom. But they could not stop the overmiserable from committing suicide.

And hard as I try, neither can I.

I can only tell the TV audience what I personally believe: "Even though suicide alone does not determine our eternal destiny, we still have to answer to God. Only God can give life and only God has a right to take it away. When we take a life, we assume the position of God. And when we go through that door and He's the first one we meet, I can imagine He might say, 'Why did you take over a role that belongs to Me?'

"I have people say, 'Chaplain, I think I'm gonna do it. I think I'm gonna kill myself.' And I say, 'Well, what are you going to say to God when you get there?'

"And when they say, 'Well, I don't know...' I tell them,

'Well, this is the time to think about it, you know, because it's too late once you pull that trigger.'"

And by now the phones are ringing, and the misery comes winging in out of the darkness, hard and fast and sore.

"About four years ago," the first caller says, "I tried to commit suicide. I overdosed on drugs. And about six weeks ago, I met a friend that I never knew I had—Jesus. Since I've met him, I'd like to share with others that He's always there. And a lot of people don't know we have this friend."

There is something fragile in her voice.

And Karen asks her, "What was going on in your life that was so bad for you that you didn't feel like living?"

"I had a child that my ex-husband took and run off with, and my father was killed in a tragic car accident and I couldn't get to the funeral..."

"You were really alone, weren't you?"

"Yes, very, very alone."

"That's one of the reasons that Harold and I appreciate your testimony about Jesus Christ always being there."

"Yes," I chime in, still worried, "but tell me, Angie, have you overcome those suicidal feelings now?"

"Yes I have. I feel, I feel good."

"Good, good."

"I'm getting baptized next week."

"Wonderful. The way you've overcome is an example for many. But I want you to know that there still may be some low times. Don't think that just because you're a Christian there won't be low times... "

And then there's Janet, a sad, disembodied, and somewhat countrified voice on the phone. Janet says she suffers from Multiple Personality Disorder (MPD) and has been thinking of killing herself.

"I've had a lot of suicidal thoughts and attempts and things, and I've been told, if that's what you feel like you have to do, you just go right ahead. But my 'System' (of alter-egos) very strongly wants me to survive...

"Because I believe there is a reason for us to be on earth. We are each God's representatives. I'm sure you'll agree that when you are down and having a difficult time and someone well-meaning says, 'All you need to do is turn your life over to Christ,' you're thinking: I'm doing that already! I'm *doing* that! Where *is* He???'"

"And that's when we need to come up to you, those of us who know you, and put our arms around you, and be your friend—in other words, *show* you Christ on earth—at that time, in that place. That's not talking it; that's doing it."

Janet thought about that for a moment. "I'm real involved in Al-Anon, and someone there said it pretty good. He said that sometimes what we need is God with skin on."

I like that: God with skin on.

That's what we need most, when it's dark.

Chapter 20

It's a strange job, delivering these death messages.

I am a Messenger of Death who tries to be a healer. I try to be your best friend at a time when I'm also your worst nightmare come true. I come into your home as a total stranger to deliver the most intimate knowledge you're likely to ever get. I come as an official, a stranger hoping to offer a personal, caring shoulder to cry on.

It is a difficult job to have to do under the best of circumstances. It's a sad job that someone has to do—and I strive to do it better each time.

Though what follows is mainly aimed at professionals (law enforcement officers, chaplains, pastors), it may also be useful to the layman: Some portions of it have relevance to every member of every family and every friend in every social circle.

Because while the police, or, in some cities, the police chaplain, may notify the wife, it may next fall to a sister to tell a brother, a brother to tell an uncle, or father; an employer to tell a close co-worker... on down the line. Each of us as a human forms the point of a huge pyramid of relationships, from close family to distant relatives to friends to co-workers to acquaintances.

How gently yet firmly and honestly we begin to spread the bad news down through the pyramid may set the tone for how others do it further on down that line. How easy we make it and how rapidly we allow the recovery process to begin is the ultimate measure of the job well done, whether we undertake it as professionals or as fathers, brothers, uncles, aunts, sisters, or sons.

Further, I have found that, in each family, there seems to be one person who is strong enough to try to take it on himself to—"take charge" of the emotional well-being of the other family members. If this person can understand the job of the professionals involved in the process, particularly "at the scene," he or she may be much better able to streamline the process for police and lessen the misery for the family by sharing that understanding.

* Remember that all deaths are difficult, and a suicide is the most difficult death possible. When talking to the family, monitor your language closely—yet without concealing or distorting the facts—so you don't cause the family further problems. The word "suicide" will probably be used by the family later, but it is NOT the time for you, the professional, to use it; it is a stigma for some. At the scene or during notification of close relatives, soften the term to, "from a self-inflicted wound," or "by his own hand."

* If it is your job as a professional to make the first notification, where possible, go in and actually view the body. Look especially at the face so that you can tell the family whether an open-casket service is going to be possible. This sounds morbid, but it is one of the family's first and automatic concerns.

Where an open-casket viewing is out of the question, try to recruit the "strong" family member to tell them they will not be able to view the body during services. Some family members will still adamantly demand to see the body immediately, as is. You should work very hard to discourage this. In my view, there is nothing to be gained from close survivors seeing badly mutilated, burned, or decomposed bodies. The scene will be eternally etched into the survivor's memories and may even manifest itself as post-traumatic stress. However, some cannot be dissuaded. If this is the case, make sure you accompany them to the viewing and are there to get them out as quickly as possible.

* Be honest. While no one is comfortable with the facts and feelings that surround a death—and especially a

suicide—the best policy is always honesty. Misinformation could confuse and later, anger members of the family.

* Be willing to accept and hear the survivors' feelings. The anger at the deceased may be more evident in some families than in others, but it will be there. Dealing with anger is the key to accepting it. Further, always strive to take a non-judgmental stance in suicides. It is not our place to judge the deceased, and certainly not our place to make our judgments available to survivors—we cannot know the suicide's inner misery or motives. Both condemnation and forgiveness lie in the hands of the survivors. We should try to make it clear that the actual decision to live or die was not in their hands but the hands of the suicide victim.

* Recognize their need for acceptance. In the case of a suicide—or, frequently in the case of victim-induced but not deliberate death—as in a drunk-driving fatality—the survivors are embarrassed and humiliated. They want to know what to say to friends and neighbors. The best thing, again, is to advise them to tell the truth; when we don't tell the truth we are entering into denial. We are in a position to impart information that will help them begin to deal with the situation honestly.

* If the survivors are Christians, they will often ask, "Did he go to hell because he committed suicide?" If they don't ask it out loud, they will ask it in their hearts. Frequently, I broach the question before it is asked by saying, "I know that one of your questions is whether he was condemned to hell because he took his own life. I have studied Scripture for forty years, and I find no place where it is said that suicide is a mortal sin and will send them to hell. It is not the way they die but how they lived and to whom they committed their life that is important." Hopefully, this attitude will give them some freedom to begin the process of forgiving the suicide.

* Help them build a support system. As a professional, you should think of yourself as only the first part of the rebuilding process for that family. The rest of the support system consists of friends, neighbors, clergy, and so on.

Find out from the bereaved who it is they wish you to
notify; get the numbers (almost everyone has an address
book; just ask them for it) and then begin notifying these
people by telephone yourself. The bereaved person is often
hysterical and will only breed hysteria on the other end
of the line; what you are seeking to build here is a network
of stability and security to support the bereaved while
they are incapacitated.

* Prayer? If the family requests it. Chaplains and
counselors who pour out a canned prayer on the survivors
are avoiding the situation rather than dealing with it.
Touching the survivors, nurturing them, helping them
build a support system, unwrangling the bureaucratic
necessities, and helping them to know what to expect in
the near future are all more helpful than canned praying.
Unless they indicate that a voiced prayer is wanted, tell
them basically, "I am sorry for your loss, and I will be
praying for you."

The things that survivors possess least of at such a time
are security and answers. This means they will be full of
questions, particularly in cases of suicide. The biggest
question is the one to which they will never have the
actual answer: Why? Why did he do that to us? The best
answer to that question is also the truest one: You will
never get the answer to why because he/she has taken
the answer with them. Of course, they will ask themselves
this question time and time again, but your reply may at
least give them the latitude to let it rest for a while.

The other major concern is always how the victim
killed himself. And the simplest language is the best. Don't
tell any more than is necessary, and don't use graphic
language. Neither, however, should you euphemize. Be
straightforward. Say things like, gunshot wound. Hanged
himself. Ran his car into a bridge.

As the notification phase winds down, the family will
begin to turn its attention toward more practical matters,
like what they should do now. This is a healthy sign
though they are by no means out of the woods, and may
not be for months or years to come. You should advise

them of the next few steps. I make it a practice to carry with me a brochure which lists the funeral homes in my town, along with their phone numbers, addresses, and a map.

I also give them a list of everything that I am telling them at this stage—for example: "Call the Medical Examiner to designate a funeral home," and so on.

The more written information the survivors have, the more real the circumstances become for them. And making it real for them is one of your responsibilities at this point. This may seem a little harsh, but remember that until it's real, they cannot begin to deal with it. Then be quick to make referrals that will plug them into survivors' groups in your area.

They may also ask questions, like, "Should we throw away his personal belongings?" Give them answers that allow choices as circumstances change. For instance, "Do that only when you feel the time is right. You may wish to keep a few personal belongings later on. You should try not to treat his room (clothes, and so on) as a monument to him. But don't give his clothes to people you know."

Another question will almost certainly be asked: "What did we do wrong?" The answer is, "Nothing. It was not your choice, not your decision."

Many suicide survivors hope to find a loophole—some consolation in the belief that the suicide was actually an accident, or a homicide. You should, as kindly as possible, close this door for them, as it may lead them only to confusion and denial. Yet, at this early stage of the investigation, you should leave yourself an out. After all, once in a while it does turn out, upon further investigation, to have been something besides suicide.

So again, the full truth is the best answer: "At this time, the best information we have is that it was self-inflicted."

Keep in mind that the job of death notification is like any other job—it is a specialty, one segment of a larger process. Notify them. Hold their hands. Counsel with them. Follow up with more counseling. Help sons and daughters work all the way through their grief and anger.

After the initial phase is through, it is not your job to take over their lives, but to steer them to counseling and other forms of support; not to *be* their lifelong guide but to get them to their lifelong friends; not to *be* their pastor, but to contact their pastor.

It is at this stage that friends and family become of paramount importance, as only they can build a support net of comfort around the bereaved. At a certain point, unless you are a miracle worker when it comes to dealing with people, your presence as a stranger will become intrusive. Survivors need their privacy and their friends.

I believe that professional counseling is very, very helpful—but the sad truth is that only about three percent of the bereaved will seek such counseling in the year following the death. This tells me that comfort comes—if it comes at all—from family and friends.

There are numerous books on the subject of survivors, but here is a thumbnail sketch of what survivors can expect—and what family and friends should prepare for, particularly in cases of suicide, since suicide is the most difficult kind of death for survivors to deal with.

The normal grief associated with any death is compounded by the fact that people can't talk about it comfortably, and that reticence gets in the way of healing. Dead is dead, but there is a world of difference between Grandma peacefully slipping away in the nursing home and Junior shooting himself in the living room. That difference is trauma—the kind that leads to post-traumatic stress syndrome (PSS).

Signs of PSS which friends and family should watch in the survivor include:

* Recurrent recollections of the event, and sometimes the feeling that the event is actually recurring in present time. Sometimes this stress manifests itself as recurring dreams.

* Prolonged feelings of numbness, coupled with a lessening of interest in important activities and a feeling of detachment from others.

* Sleep disturbances, trouble concentrating, loss of memory, guilt about surviving. Sometimes sufferers are easily startled and may carefully avoid activities that may remind them of the trauma.

Trying to deal with PSS alone makes getting over it that much harder, as does having no chance to talk to others about the experience, the guilt, the shame and the silence. To the extent that you can listen, you can help.

There are other aspects of suicide of which friends, as part of a survivors' support system, need to be aware.

First, there is no death more sudden, from the survivors' standpoint, than suicide. It is the one possibility for which most of us are never prepared.

When an automobile accident causes a fatality, there is already some rudimentary "preparatory awareness" in place. You know deep down that anyone who drives a car, including you, could be involved in such an accident.

Similarly, death by homicide is hugely shocking to survivors—but homicides are on the nightly news; they are not unheard of, and, further, do not involve the *deceased* having any "intent" towards you.

When natural death occurs, some groundwork for preparing survivors for a death by illness, even when premature, has been done as an integral part of the healing process—medicines, doctors, and hospitals all serve as tacit warning that there might be a fatal problem around the corner, and visiting with the sick person usually allows survivors to have at least partial closure.

But for suicide survivors, the predominant feelings are shock, surprise, and the feeling that they have been rejected in the most meaningful sense possible, and furthermore, rejected without consultation. The suicide victim chose to do it IN SPITE of loving family and friends.

This is a truly stunning, debilitating blow, and may leave the survivors rudderless in life. How can they face life? How can they deal with their jobs?

They are initially at a loss.

Later, anger will begin to creep into their feelings: Anger over the perceived desertion; anger over not being allowed to help; anger over the suicide's almost casual rejection of life—and, perhaps most importantly, there will be guilt over that anger.

If there is one pervasive reaction common to suicide survivors, it is guilt. And, since the suicide took to the grave the full truth about what was responsible for his misery and his decision, the survivors' imaginations run wild with questions about whether they bear some of the responsibility.

This tendency may become extreme to the point of being ridiculous to everyone except the sufferer. But you cannot, in dealing with someone who is going through this, assume that you can merely correct them and that will solve the problem; they must reach the point where they can see these things themselves.

There is also the shame and the feelings of "apartness" from the rest of society that are engendered by the suicide. Part of this is based on beliefs that suicide runs in the family, part of it stems from self-consciousness. But much of it stems from the silence of others.

People are uncomfortable about suicide. They think that they are trying to spare the survivors' feelings about it, when in fact by their silence they are confirming the survivors' worst fear—that it's just too disgusting and awful to talk about.

Another very human and understandable reaction to suicide is to develop anxiety about the other survivors. The shadow of death has passed over their lives. What once seemed stable and reliable has proven ephemeral. They feel that they can never again trust the world to treat them kindly or predictably.

This plethora of miseries and mis-emotion sometimes totals up to the Big Misery—long-lasting depression. Some depression is to be expected, of course. But depression tends to further its own end. Depressed people neglect relationships and jobs, getting them into further trouble, which is further cause for depression. They don't call people, and soon people stop calling them, thus "confirming" their lack of self-esteem. Without intervention and care, this may lead to that worst of survivor tragedies: Another suicide.

In fact, this tendency toward self-destructive thinking is so widespread in survivors that some self-help groups refer to these suicidal feelings as, sad to say, "normal." Hardly any intimate survivor escapes the impulse. Usually it is not acted upon—but the fear, for the survivor, can be debilitating.

Unfortunately, while it is obvious that more suicides may follow one, it is not as clear how to successfully predict which individuals in a suicide-stricken family are most at risk. But there are some factors which "support-net" members should at least be on the lookout for.

Does the survivor idolize the dead person? If the idolatry is extreme, he may wish to follow the ultimate example. Did the suicidal one have sufficient familial rank and authority and respect to leave the impression among survivors that suicide is somehow "sanctioned" as an option in dealing with problems? Does the survivor demonstrate uncharacteristic violence—destroying his own property in a fit of rage, or injuring himself? That violence and anger may be turned inward at some point.

Does the survivor act out "sacrificial" behavior—for example, taking an unrepresentative delight in doing the grubby chores no one seems to want or being the butt of humiliating jokes? Has self-deprecation exceeded the bounds of modesty? It could be a form of self-punishment, of penance for imagined sins against the dead.

The reverberations from suicide echo and ripple for so many years that one might as well say they go on forever. Long after the stronger emotions have passed, the lives of survivors are forever altered in subtler ways. To go on living, it seems that each survivor feels the need to make some kind of deal or accommodation with the suicide or his memory:

Since there is usually no chance to tell the suicidal person goodbye, that lack of closure with the deceased can become pathological. Instead of saying "Goodbye forever," he becomes someone who is forever saying goodbye.

That was my fear concerning Linda Christiansen; that she was trying to keep her son, Craig, alive by living her own life as a memorial to him. The healthy signs in her case were that she seemed to focus most of her hopes on her new son and remaining daughter.

It is normal to wish to "always remember," but to the extent that it prevents you from living your own life, it can be unhealthy.

There is no clear means of distinguishing when love has turned to obsession, but the question ought to be at least raised if:

—The possessions or the living quarters of the deceased are viewed as sacrosanct, and kept just as they were during the deceased's life.

—If the survivor tries to turn all occasions into an excuse for everyone to remember the deceased.

—If the survivor begins to manifest intense interest in other deaths and memorial observances with little regard to the distance of the relationship with the deceased.

People like Linda Christiansen build their mental memorial out of good moments, at least; in far worse shape are those survivors who try themselves, find themselves guilty, and accept as their eternal punishment a lifelong rehearsal of bad moments in which they had a hand during the life of the deceased.

Persons suffering this kind of guilt are basically trying to pay off their perceived obligation to the deceased by becoming victims themselves—victims of guilt. This guilt also helps them to refrain from committing the "sin" of being angry at the deceased, and it is, of course, very self-fulfilling; if it's guilt you are looking for, you can always find it in ANY relationship.

Then there is the matter of blame. Many survivors, choked by the anger they feel toward themselves and the person who committed suicide, are unable to face the emotion. They are also reluctant to "tarnish the memory" of the deceased by facing and acknowledging that the suicide occurred because the victim willed it. They deny it, and find outlets and scapegoats for it that are unreasonable or inappropriate. They may blame the doctor who "failed" to diagnose depression when he was asked to set a broken finger. Or the teacher who failed to see that the rebelliousness was depression. Or the ex-husband in the bad marriage.

A little bit of blame may be normal. Clearly, in many suicides, there is a precipitant, a triggering event or circumstance—most often, a relationship gone bad. To recognize, as an example, an estranged girlfriend's rejection of the deceased as a precipitant may be a matter of recognizing a segment of the truth. To assign her full blame and eternal responsibility, however, is a delusion and an evasion of the truth.

In many circumstances, the bereaved family unit itself may be the best "support group" for dealing with its own problems. Where there is an atmosphere of love and communication, sisters, brothers, fathers and mothers can talk out their grief, guilt, blame, and shame in an intimate and open atmosphere that few counselors could readily or rapidly create.

But one problem that occasionally arises is that this network of mutual support tacitly agrees on a game plan for surviving a suicide that is actually damaging to all involved. They agree to NOT deal with the death and the damage, and enter instead into a conspiracy of silence and denial. They may choose to hide—and to help each other hide—behind a multitude of evasions: that the death was actually a murder, or an accident, or at least the result of behavior so bizarre that the perpetrator can no longer be considered the "same person" they knew before the suicide.

The reasons for this denial and silence may seem sound to the survivors. After all, it puts a lid on emotions that, to a more or less "dysfunctional" family, may seem more dangerous and destructive than dismissing the death from discussion; talking about it may lead them to exposing emotions they consider ugly—guilt, blame, anger. They may also want to avoid any disruptions, and grieving IS a disruptive process.

But taking this tack both thwarts and prolongs the process of working through mourning and ultimately of letting go of all the emotions attendant upon the loss.

The conspiracy of silence also allows erroneous misconceptions, irrational guilts, and misplaced anger to take root in each individual, sometimes with awful consequences. This silence allows all the other negative consequences—delusions, denial, depression, guilt, blame, self-destructiveness, depression—to flourish unchecked.

Sadly, the American public seems all too ready to support survivors in their silence. There may be real—or, equally damaging, imagined—disdain from friends, neighbors and clergy. Even the noncommittal, poker-faced attitude of some policemen investigating the death may be seen as accusatory. Well-meaning friends, wishing to refrain from bringing up an unpleasant subject, may unwittingly support the family's belief that discussion of the suicide is a social faux pas.

And there seems to be a million old maxims supporting them in their decision to keep quiet, along the lines of letting sleeping dogs lie and not opening old wounds. Survivors need to realize that the dogs may look like they're lying very still, but they're really wide awake, and the wounds may have stopped bleeding but they're far from healed.

You won't do any good by dragging it out of them, but you should try to create an environment in which they can let it out when it's time. Unfortunately, the truth for humans is the same as that in physics; for every action, a reaction; for every bottled pressure, sooner or later an outlet. The anger and guilt will find some outlet besides verbal catharsis, and it may be damaging, inappropriate, or even self-destructive.

The point for survivors is that they *should* talk until they are blue in the face if that's what it takes—to other family members, if that's what works, and to friends, professionals and other survivors if it doesn't. But survivors should also remember that nobody can *make* them talk.

The ultimate responsibility for the survivors' well-being

must be taken by the survivors themselves. Nobody can live through it for them, nobody can make the choices they need to make, and certainly nobody can say what it is that they need to say or face the facts that need facing. Effectively dealing with the grief with the aim of diminishing it over time is by no means the same thing as "forgetting" the deceased or "diminishing" his memory, by coping with it.

The aim of recovery is not so much to get survivors completely over the loss (which is probably impossible anyway) but rather to help them reach a point where there is room for pleasant thoughts about the deceased, rather than guilt and blame; to get them to the point where they can realize, emotionally and intellectually, that they are not responsible for the suicide. In short, to help them get back to their own world, to a place where they can feel good about themselves again. The dead have lived their lives; the living must continue to live theirs.

Some survivors believe that by "being over it next week" they trivialize the deceased. There is no danger here. In the first place, they may not be substantially "over it" by next year and may for the rest of their lives have relapses and recurrences. So the sooner they seek help, the sooner they may be restored to effective living.

Survivors also should realize it isn't ever fun. They will feel rotten; everybody who has ever lost someone they loved to suicide can expect misery aplenty. There is no need to go looking for it, no need to add to it—and every reason and right in the world to speak up about it, acknowledge it, and begin to deal with it.

They should know also that many people do not complete the mourning process but instead become "stuck" at some point. It's part of the package. If this happens, they should seek help. Suicide is perhaps the stickiest death on earth for survivors, and sometimes it takes some help getting unstuck.

Further, survivors should not let anyone tell them how they should feel. Each case is different, and the order in which the emotions (and combinations of emotions) descend upon them is entirely individual. They should take the emotions as they come, and deal with them as they can.

Perhaps most of all, survivors need to know they are not alone—and that suicide is not nearly so rare nor remarkable as our society has led us to believe. If they want evidence of this, they should try checking the obituary column of your local paper. They will probably never find the word "suicide." Most survivors, understandably, don't want it known that their relative killed himself.

Every so often, however, a survivor will be determined to get the truth into the local paper. But unless the victim is someone of notoriety, the survivor faces an uphill battle. I know of only one survivor who has fought this battle and won. She gave a brief written obituary to the paper in which she mentioned that her daughter had killed herself. Pretty soon her phone was ringing, and the panicked newspaperman on the other end said, "Are you SURE you want to say suicide?"

"Yes."

"Well, you know, you could say a brief illness..."

"She killed herself."

"Well, we could just leave out the cause of death..."

"But she killed herself. I think the people who knew her ought to know."

"Well, you probably need to speak to my boss, then..."

Policies vary from paper to paper—but they tend to err on the side of fearfulness. Beyond the obituary pages, on the news side, the caution is even greater; you will not likely read about the suicide of the man who jumped off the skyscraper into downtown traffic for fear that it will encourage others to seek publicity the same way.

Perhaps this fear is valid, but one of the results is that, in the public consciousness, suicide is seen as such a rarity that, when it occurs within a family, it worsens the burden by adding a feeling of separateness from the rest of the community.

So one of the steps the survivor may need to take, on

his own, is locating other victims. Most county or metropolitan health departments maintain an extensive list of local organizations, which will likely include a chapter of Survivors of Suicide. You don't have to be crazy to call MHMR. In fact, keeping people from becoming that way is one of their primary missions.

Survivors also need to be aware that, within reasonable limits, whatever negative emotion they are feeling is "OK," at least as far as reflecting normalcy.

Loss? That person is gone, and isn't coming back. Let nobody tell survivors that one of these days they'll look back on their feelings and laugh—but someday they might be able to look back on the person, or something he said or did, and laugh at the fondness of the memory.

Depression? Of course survivors are depressed. One source of relief for many is simply finding something— almost anything, in fact—to do with their time; something to get them back into the flow of life.

One of the first and simplest bits of "doing" may be the most important: Getting involved in memorial or funeral services for the deceased. Too many families try to dodge this bullet, allowing their shame and hurt and rage to cause them to avoid a funeral or memorial service.

One thing I tell these families is that they are not going through the funeral or memorial service for the deceased, but for themselves, to begin the process of grief. They are not marking the horror of the means of death, but mourning the magnitude of the loss of the living—of that which was good and valuable.

Further, neglecting this may later add to their already heavy burden of guilt. "He was miserable enough to kill himself in spite of all we did—and then we didn't even give him a decent burial." I have talked to more than a few families who thought they didn't want a memorial service into having one anyway; invariably, they have later thanked me.

It's also helpful to help others, particularly those in the same situation. That is why groups such as Survivors of Suicide are often helpful. By offering a shoulder to cry on, survivors may feel that they've earned the right to ASK for one to cry on.

Other benefits are obvious—nobody understands like someone who's been there. Their experiences and insights may spark survivors to some insights of their own. Grief shared as a group rather than endured alone seems to somehow "officialize" it and thus acknowledge it. Also, there are in such groups people at all stages of the recovery process. Some may serve as role models for the recently bereaved, while others may see *them* as role models— which cannot help but improve their self-esteem.

(The only word of warning I would add concerns the modern and somewhat over-inclusive assumption that everyone is "in processing" in one way or another; and the corollary is that no one can "really" recover. In many groups there is often someone who is more interested in convincing a newcomer that they are ill rather than in helping them recover. Common sense should prevail.)

Guilt? If they feel it they feel it. The most "recovered" people are those who can more or less confidently reject the notion that they were responsible for the death of their loved one—or who have at least placed limits on that responsibility. That's something to shoot for, but it can't be expected to happen overnight or even necessarily by the next year.

Angry? You bet they are. To the extent that they can discharge this rage (appropriately), they can overcome it. That is why many therapists recommend yelling at the deceased as though he were present. Let him have it. Survivors wouldn't be mad if they didn't love the deceased.

Uncertainty? It's natural. After all, a major event has disrupted the survivors' lives.

Survivors have learned that some people kill themselves; they also need to be open to relearning an even more important lesson: Most people DON'T.

Most survivors express the hope that no one should ever have to suffer as they have, and some say they would do anything to help prevent that. But they can't help anyone if they remain basket cases. Their hard-won in-depth knowledge—of both why suicide needs preventing, and how to survive it when it isn't—is greatly needed.

So, please, help us.

Suicide is not painless. It is a fatal mistake that produces ripples of destruction for generations yet unborn.

Appendix

Some warning signs of unmanageable stress or depression in adolescents include:

* Prolonged sadness.

* Extremes of mood, particularly between indifference, manic talkativeness, and eagerness.

* Sudden rages and verbal attacks.

* Hypersensitivity and overreaction to criticism.

* Perfectionism, and the resulting feeling that they cannot live up to their own expectations.

* Ambivalence between dependence and independence.

* Complaints concerning the emptiness or meaninglessness of living.

* Restless agitation.

* Rebelliousness and uncooperativeness.

* Sleep disturbances.

* Increased or decreased appetite and sudden weight gain or loss.

* Inexplicable physical symptoms, such as headaches with no physical cause.

* Chronic fatigue.

These are signs of depression, not necessarily of impending suicide. They should be monitored closely, of course. There are some more serious signs that may indicate a need to hit the panic button. These include:

* Overt expressions of death wishes, suicide ideas, or plans.

* Verbal clues. Sometimes these are as overt as, "Think I'll just go kill myself." Most are a shade more subtle,

such as, "Don't worry about my English grade, it won't be a problem much longer."

* Marked accident-proneness. They may not be accidents at all; he may be working his way up to greater heights of self-destruction.

* "Completing arrangements." A teenager who suddenly seems compelled to finish up extended personal projects, or, more alarming still, to part with prized possessions, may be "putting his affairs in order," and if so, is at critical risk for suicide.

* Blowing savings on shopping sprees or compulsive travel, as though trying to cram lots of fun into "the time left."

* Compulsive and unwavering interest in perceived rejections by authority figures or peer groups.

* Undue fascination with past "sins" and attempts to atone for them.

* Wild exhilaration on the heels of extended gloom. This may indicate relief from having reached a firm decision to take the final step.

Bibliography

We are grateful to several authors whose scholarship greatly informed our thinking and which are invaluable resources for any serious student of suicidology. We particularly wish to acknowledge (and heartily recommend) Alfred Alverez and his *The Savage God* (Random House, 1972) for his far-reaching and eminently readable accounts on the psychology, philosophy, and history of suicide, and the role literature has played in its progression through the ages. While there are many books on the subject, Alvarez' is the best; he brought to his work an unusual sense of perspective, poetry, and understanding. *The Savage God* is a must both for the layman looking for a good book and any student of suicide.

For many facts on suicide and survivorship we gratefully acknowledge:

Fatal Choice: The Teenage Suicide Crisis, John Q. Baucom, Moody Press, 1986;

What You Should Know About Suicide, Bill Blackburn, Word Books, 1982;

The Case Against Suicide, William V. Rauscher, St Martin's Press, 1981;

Cry For Help, Norman Farberow and Edwin Shneidman, Blakiston Div., McGraw Hill, 1961;

Suicide: The Gamble with Death, Gene Lester, Prentice-Hall, 1971;

(Continued next page)

Survivors of Suicide, Albert C. Cain, Thomas Books, 1972;
Traitor Within: Our Suicide Problem, Edward Robb Ellis, Doubleday, 1961;
Silent Grief: Living in the Wake of Suicide, Christopher Lukas, 1987;

For information supporting our contentions concerning the evolution of embalming and cemeteries:

Inventing the American Way of Death, James J. Farrell, Temple University Press;
The American Way of Death, Jessica Mitford, Simon and Schuster, 1963.

And for our reconstruction of the "suicide epidemic" of the 1980's, we would like to thank *The Dallas Morning News*.

A MESSAGE FROM THE PUBLISHER

W. R. Spence, M.D.
Publisher

Harold Elliott has a most unusual personality for a suicide chaplain. On the surface he's a natural comic and total optimist. But when the subject turns to suicide, especially among adolescents, Elliott is all seriousness and sensitivity. The nurturing nature of his years as a pastor immediately came through to me when I first met him, and I believe his readers will sense his message that suicide is indeed not painless.

While it is often easy to turn a profit with stories of greed, sex and violence, we at WRS Publishing are not interested in these kind of books. We only produce books we can be proud of—books that focus on people and or issues that enlighten and inspire—books that can change lives for the better. **Call us at 1-800-299-3366 for suggestions or for a free book catalog.**

WRS
PUBLISHING
A Division of WRS Group, Inc.
Waco, Texas